*Law*Basics

EVIDENCE

By

David H. Sheldon, LL.B. (Hons.), Dip. L.P.

Pupil Advocate;
Lecturer in Private Law, University of Edinburgh

EDINBURGH
W. GREEN/Sweet & Maxwell
1998

First published 1998

Published in 1998 by W. Green & Son Limited of
21 Alva Street,
Edinburgh, EH2 4PS

Typeset by Trinity Typesetting,
Edinburgh

Printed in Great Britain by
The Cromwell Press, Trowbridge, Wiltshire

No natural forests were destroyed to make this product; only farmed timber was
used and replanted

A CIP catalogue record of this book is available from the British Library

ISBN 0 414 01236 4

CONTENTS

	Page
Table of Cases	vii
1. Introduction	1
2. Relevance	4
3. The Burden of Proof	6
4. Presumptions	10
5. The Standard of Proof	13
6. Sufficiency of Evidence	15
7. Admissibility of Evidence	22
8. Witnesses	70
9. Civil Evidence	76
10. Appeals	80
Appendix: Sample Examination Questions and Answer Plans	84
Index	97

*Law*Basics

EVIDENCE

Available soon:

Other titles in the Series

Agency
Constitutional Law
Delict

TABLE OF CASES

	Page
A v. B (1895) 22 R. 402	46, 47
A.B. v. Glasgow and West of Scotland Blood Transfusion Service, 1993 S.L.T. 36	66
Abadom (1982) 76 Crim.App.R. 48	57
Adair v. McGarry, 1933 J.C. 72	35
Admiralty v. Aberdeen Steam Trawling and Fishing Co., 1909 S.C. 335	64
Advocate, H.M. v. Brotherston, 1995 S.C.C.R. 613	76
— v. Cairns, 1967 J.C. 37	69
— v. Campbell, 1964 J.C. 80	43, 89
— v. Cumming, 1983 S.C.C.R. 15	34
— v. Davie (1881) 4 Coup. 450	63
— v. Gilgannon, 1983 S.C.C.R. 10	42
— v. Harper, 1987 S.C.C.R. 472	37
— v. Hepper, 1958 J.C. 39	35
— v. Joseph, 1929 J.C. 55	47, 48
— v. Kay, 1970 J.C. 68	50
— v. McGuigan, 1936 J.C. 16	36, 37
— v. Mair, 1982 S.L.T. 471	40
— v. Mitchell, 1951 J.C. 53	15
— v. Monson (1893) 21 R. (J.) 5	30, 93
— v. Parker, 1944 J.C. 49	64
— v. Pender, 1996 S.C.C.R. 404	39
— v. Turnbull, 1951 J.C. 96	35
Advocate's, Lord, Reference (No. 1 of 1983), 1984 S.L.T. 337	39, 40
Advocate's, Lord, Reference (No. 1 of 1992), 1992 S.L.T. 1010	28, 84, 86, 92, 93
Air Canada v. Secretary of State for Trade [1983] 2 A.C. 396	66
Alexander (W.) & Sons v. Dundee Corporation, 1950 S.C. 123	5, 46, 47
Anderson v. Laverock, 1976 J.C. 9	23
Anderson (William) v. J. B. Fraser & Co. Ltd, 1992 S.C.L.R. 417	79
Argyll, Duke of v. Duchess of Argyll, 1963 S.L.T. 42	45
Auld v. McBey (1881) 18 S.L.R. 312	74
B v. Kennedy, 1987 S.L.T. 765	14
Baird v. Mitchell (1854) 16 D. 1088	60
Balloch v. H.M. Advocate, 1977 J.C. 23	44
Bater v. Bater [1951] P. 35	14
Bates v. H.M. Advocate, 1989 S.L.T. 701	73
Baxter v. Scott, 1992 S.C.C.R. 342	36
Beattie v. H.M. Advocate, 1995 S.L.T. 275	83, 84
Bell v. Lothiansure Ltd, 1990 S.L.T. 58	65
Binnie v. Rederij Theodoro B.V., 1993 S.C. 71	61
Bird v. Bird, 1931 S.C. 731	73
Birkett v. H.M. Advocate, 1992 S.C.C.R. 850	76
Black v. Annan, 1995 S.C.C.R. 273	44, 89
Blagojevic v. H.M. Advocate, 1995 S.C.C.R. 570	42, 56, 57
Brady v. H.M. Advocate, 1986 S.C.C.R. 191	50
Bremner v. H.M. Advocate, 1992 S.C.C.R. 476	51, 96
Brims v. MacDonald, 1993 S.C.C.R. 1061	59
Brown v. Glen, 1997 S.C.C.R. 636	38
— v. Rolls Royce, 1960 S.C. (H.L.) 22	9
Buchan (John) and Malcolm Maclean (1833) Bell's Notes 293	75
Buchanan v. Price, 1982 S.C.C.R. 534	8
Burke v. Wilson, 1988 S.C.C.R. 361	34

Byrne *v.* Ross, 1993 S.L.T. 307 77

Carberry *v.* H.M. Advocate, 1975 J.C. 40 52
Carpenter *v.* Hamilton, 1994 S.C.C.R. 108 21
Casey *v.* H.M. Advocate, 1993 S.L.T. 33 .... 72, 73
Chalmers *v.* H.M. Advocate, 1954 J.C. 66 .... 38, 39, 40
Chassar *v.* Macdonald, 1996 S.C.C.R. 730 34
Church *v.* H.M. Advocate, 1995 S.L.T. 604 83
Codona *v.* H.M. Advocate, 1996 S.C.C.R. 300 .... 39, 42, 44, 89
Coffey *v.* Houston, 1992 S.L.T. 520 21
Comerford *v.* Strathclyde R.C., 1987 S.C.L.R. 758 77
Conoco (U.K.) Ltd *v.* The Commercial Law Practice, 1997 S.L.T. 372 63
Constantine (Joseph) Steamship Line Ltd *v.* Imperial Smelting Corporation Ltd
   [1942] A.C. 154 7
Conway *v.* Rimmer [1968] A.C. 910 66
Cordiner *v.* H.M. Advocate, 1978 J.C. 64 52
Custerton *v.* Westwater, 1987 S.C.C.R. 389 41

Daks Simpson Group plc *v.* Kuiper, 1994 S.L.T. 689 65
Daniels, 1960, unreported 64
Davidson *v.* Brown, 1990 J.C. 324 37
Davie *v.* Magistrates of Edinburgh, 1953 S.C. 34 .... 55, 56, 58
Davies *v.* Maguire, 1995 S.L.T. 755 80
Deb *v.* Normand, 1996 S.C.C.R. 766 23
Devine *v.* Colvilles, 1969 S.L.T. 154 13
Devlin *v.* Normand, 1992 S.C.C.R. 875 37
Dickie *v.* H.M. Advocate (1897) 2 Adam 331 .... 50, 51, 94, 95
Dickson *v.* Minister of Pensions [1953] 1 Q.B. 228 7
Donaldson *v.* Valentine, 1996 S.C.C.R. 374 59
Donnelly *v.* Carmichael, 1996 S.L.T. 153 60
Drummond *v.* H.M. Advocate, 1992 S.C.C.R. 290 35
Dumoulin *v.* H.M. Advocate, 1974 S.L.T. (Notes) 42 48

Earnshaw *v.* H.M. Advocate, 1981 S.C.C.R. 279 8
Edinburgh District Council *v.* MacDonald, 1979 S.L.T. (Sh. Ct.) 58 12
Elliot *v.* H.M. Advocate, 1995 S.L.T. 612 83
— *v.* Joicey, 1935 S.C. (H.L.) 57 60

F *v.* Kennedy (No. 2), 1992 S.C.L.R. 750 .... 78, 79, 90, 91, 92
Farrans *v.* Roxburghe C.C., 1969 S.L.T. 35 68
Forrester *v.* H.M. Advocate, 1952 J.C. 28 58
Foster *v.* H.M. Advocate, 1932 J.C. 75 73
Fox *v.* H.M. Advocate, 1998 S.L.T. 335 17
— *v.* Patterson, 1948 J.C. 104 12
Frew *v.* Jessop, 1990 S.L.T. 396 31
Friel, Petr., 1981 S.C. 1 66

G's Trs. *v.* G, 1936 S.C. 837 12
Gallagher *v.* Paton, 1909 S.C. (J.) 50 47
Gibson *v.* BICC, 1973 S.C. (H.L.) 15 3
— *v.* NCR, 1925 S.C. 500 9
Gillespie *v.* Macmillan, 1957 J.C. 31 .... 6, 86–87
Gilmour *v.* H.M. Advocate, 1982 S.C.C.R. 590 .... 19, 90
Glaser *v.* Glaser, 1997 S.L.T. 456 .... 78, 91
Glasgow and South Western Ry *v.* Boyd and Forrest, 1918 S.C. (H.L.) 14 69
Glasgow Corporation *v.* The Central Land Board, 1956 S.C. (H.L.) 1 66
Glasgow Shipowners *v.* Clyde Navigation Trustees (1885) 12 R. 695 68
Glebe Sugar Refining Co., The *v.* The Trustees of the Port and Harbours of Greenock,
   1921 S.C. (H.L.) 72 60

Graham *v.* H.M. Advocate, 1983 S.C.C.R. 314 52
— *v.* —, 1991 S.L.T. 416 .... 42, 43, 44, 89
— *v.* Orr, 1995 S.C.C.R. 30 36
Grahame *v.* Secretary of State for Scotland, 1951 S.C. 368 68

H *v.* P (1905) 8 F. 232 .... 47, 49, 50
H *v.* Sweeney, 1983 S.L.T. 48 69
Hamilton *v.* H.M. Advocate, 1938 J.C. 134 83
Harley *v.* H.M. Advocate, 1995 S.C.C.R. 595 44
Harris *v.* F, 1991 S.L.T. 242 .... 14, 77
Hartley *v.* H.M. Advocate, 1979 S.L.T. 26 .... 18, 39
Hay *v.* H.M. Advocate, 1968 J.C. 40 35
Hendry *v.* Clan Line Steamers, 1949 S.C. 320 14
— *v.* H.M. Advocate, 1986 S.L.T. 186 29
— *v.* —, 1987 J.C. 63 .... 54, 58
Herkes *v.* Dickie, 1958 J.C. 51 60
Higgins *v.* Burton, 1968 S.L.T. (Notes) 52 66
— *v.* H.M. Advocate, 1993 S.C.C.R. 542 42
Highland Venison Market Ltd *v.* Allwild GmbH, 1992 S.C.L.R. 415 79
Hopes and Lavery *v.* H.M. Advocate, 1960 J.C. 104 .... 43, 57
Houston *v.* McLeod, 1986 S.C.C.R. 219 23
Howden *v.* H.M. Advocate, 1994 S.C.C.R. 23 .... 21, 22
Hunter *v.* H.M. Advocate, 1984 J.C. 90 .... 64, 73
Hynds *v.* Hynds, 1966 S.C. 201 .... 68, 69

Imre *v.* Mitchell, 1958 S.C. 439 .... 12, 13
Indian Calvary Club Ltd and Another, 1997, unreported 15
Ingram *v.* Macari, 1983 J.C. 1 54
Inland Revenue *v.* Glasgow Police Athletic Association, 1953 S.C. (H.L.) 57 60
Inland Revenue, Commissioners of *v.* Russell 1955 S.C. 237 59
Ireland *v.* Russell, 1995 S.L.T. 1348 34

Jamieson *v.* Annan, 1988 S.C.C.R. 278 .... 43, 44
— *v.* H.M. Advocate (No. 2), 1994 S.C.C.R. 610 .... 30, 31
Johnston *v.* H.M. Advocate, 1993 S.C.C.R. 693 39
— *v.* Johnston, 1996 S.L.T. 499 14
Jones *v.* Owen (1870) 34 J.P. 759 32

K *v.* Kennedy, 1992 S.C.L.R. 386 .... 75, 77, 78
K.P. *v.* H.M. Advocate, 1991 S.C.C.R. 933 75
Kelly *v.* Docherty, 1991 S.C.C.R. 312 74
Kennedy *v.* Smith and Ansvar Insurance Ltd, 1976 S.L.T. 110 59
Kenny *v.* Tudhope, 1984 S.C.C.R. 290 56
Kerr *v.* H.M. Advocate, 1958 J.C. 14 79
King *v.* Lees, 1993 S.L.T. 1184 .... 10, 15
Knutzen *v.* Mauritzen, 1918 1 S.L.T. 85 47
Kolbin and Sons *v.* Kinnear, 1930 S.C. (H.L.) 57 60

L, *Re* [1997] A.C. 16 63
L *v.* L, 1996 S.L.T. 767 .... 74, 77, 78, 79, 80
— *v.* —, 1997 S.C.L.R. 866 .... 77, 80, 92
Langan *v.* H.M. Advocate, 1989 S.C.C.R. 389 17
Lamb *v.* Lord Advocate, 1976 S.L.T. 151 12
Lambie *v.* H.M. Advocate, 1973 J.C. 53 10
Langan *v.* H.M. Advocate, 1989 S.C.C.R. 379 .... 6, 17
Lawrie *v.* Muir, 1950 J.C. 19 .... 33, 34, 45
Leckie *v.* Miln, 1982 S.L.T. 177 .... 36, 38
Lee *v.* NCB, 1955 S.C. 438 60
Leggate *v.* H.M. Advocate, 1988 S.C.C.R. 391 53

Lennon v. Co-operative Insurance Society, 1985 S.L.T. 98 14
Lennox v. NCB, 1955 S.C. 438 60
Lindsay v. H.M. Advocate, 1994 S.L.T. 546 21
Little v. H.M. Advocate, 1983 S.C.C.R. 56 .... 6, 17
Livingstone v. Murrays (1830) 9 S. 161 64
Lockhart v. Stainbridge, 1989 S.C.C.R. 220 56
Lockwood v. Walker, 1910 S.C. (J.) 3 17
London and Edinburgh Shipping Co. v. The Admiralty, 1920 S.C. 309 61
Low v. H.M. Advocate, 1993 S.C.C.R. 493 .... 19, 90

M v. Ferguson, 1994 S.C.L.R. 488 .... 75, 79
— v. Kennedy, 1993 S.C.L.R. 69 .... 58, 74, 77, 78, 92
McAllister v. Normand, 1996 S.L.T. 622 4
McArthur v. Organon Laboratories, 1982 S.L.T. 425 77
McAvoy v. Jessop, 1988 S.C.C.R. 127 35
McCallum v. British Railways Board, 1989 S.L.T. 296 77
McCann v. Adair, 1951 J.C. 127 59
McCarron v. Allen, 1988 S.C.C.R. 9 34
McCourtney v. H.M. Advocate, 1977 J.C. 68 52
McCowan v. Wright (1852) 15 D. 229 .... 62, 63
McCuaig v. H.M. Advocate, 1982 S.L.T. 383 52
McDonald v. H.M. Advocate, 1987 S.C.C.R. 581 .... 19, 90
Macdonald v. H.M. Advocate, 1989 S.C.C.R. 559 12
McDonald v. Scott, 1993 S.C.C.R. 78 17
McGinley and Dowds v. MacLeod, 1963 J.C. 11 72
McGovern v. H.M. Advocate, 1950 J.C. 33 .... 37, 38
McGowan v. Belling, 1983 S.L.T. 77 24
McIlveny v. Donald, 1995 S.C.L.R. 802 .... 24, 25, 80
Macintosh v. NCB, 1988 S.L.T. 348 81
Maciver v. McKenzie, 1942 J.C. 51 23
McKellar v. Normand, 1992 S.C.C.R. 393 23
Mackenzie v. H.M. Advocate, 1995 S.C.C.R. 14 83
— v. MacLean, 1981 S.L.T. 2 69
McLaren v. Caldwell's Paper Mills, 1973 S.L.T. 158 .... 77, 81, 91
— v. McLeod, 1913 S.C.(J.) 61 .... 26, 27, 28, 86
McLay v. H.M. Advocate, 1994 S.L.T. 873 .... 30, 85, 92–94
McLeod v. Fraser, 1986 S.C.C.R. 271 23
— v. Lowe, 1993 S.L.T. 471 26
Macleod v. Woodmuir Miners Welfare Society Social Club, 1961 J.C. 5 23
McLory v. McInnes, 1992 S.L.T. 501 42
MacNeill v. McGregor, 1975 J.C. 55 61
McPhee v. Heatherwick, 1977 S.L.T. (Sh.Ct.) 46 68
McRae v. H.M. Advocate, 1975 J.C. 34 21
McVinnie v. McVinnie, 1995 S.C.L.R. 480 .... 78, 91, 92
Main v. Andrew Wormald Ltd, 1988 S.L.T. 141 57
Mair v. H.M. Advocate, 1997 S.C.C.R. 44 20
Mallett v. McMonagle [1970] A.C. 166 14
Manuel v. H.M. Advocate, 1958 J.C. 41 .... 19, 90
Marks and Spencer v. British Gas Corporation, 1983 S.L.T. 196 64
Masih [1986] Crim.L.R. 395 56
Mathieson v. H.M. Advocate, 1996 S.C.C.R. 388 29
Melon v. Hector Powe, 1980 S.C. 188 81
Meredith v. Lees, 1992 S.L.T. 802 .... 18, 20
Micosta S.A. v. Shetland Islands Council, 1983 S.L.T. 483 63
Middler v. H.M. Advocate, 1994 S.C.C.R. 838 41
Milford v. H.M. Advocate, 1973 S.L.T. 12 35
Miller v. Minister of Pensions [1947] 63 T.L.R. 474 15
Miln v. Cullen, 1967 J.C. 21 .... 32, 39, 41, 89
Mitchell v. Dean, 1979 J.C. 62 52

— *v.* H.M. Advocate, 1996 S.C.C.R. 97 .... 19, 90
Montgomerie & Co *v.* Wallace-James (1903) 6 F. (H.L.) 10 81
Moorov *v.* H.M. Advocate, 1930 J.C. 68 .... 20–21, 47
More *v.* Brown & Root Wimpey Highland Fabricators Ltd, 1983 S.L.T. 669 65
Morrison *v.* H.M. Advocate, 1990 J.C. 299 .... 27, 29
— *v.* J. Kelly & Sons, 1970 S.C. 65 .... 77, 78, 81, 91, 92
— *v.* Mackenzie, 1990 J.C. 185 23
Morton *v.* H.M. Advocate, 1938 J.C. 50 .... 27, 83, 87
Muldoon *v.* Herron, 1970 J.C. 30 .... 30–32, 75
Mullan *v.* Anderson, 1993 S.L.T. 835 .... 14, 69
Murray *v.* Seath, 1939 S.L.T. 348 68

Namyslak *v.* H.M. Advocate, 1994 S.C.C.R. 140 35
Nelson *v.* H.M. Advocate, 1994 S.C.C.R. 192 49
— *v.* Nelson, 1994 S.C.C.R. 192 71
Nimmo *v.* Alexander Cowan and Son Ltd, 1967 S.C. (H.L.) 79 7
Norval *v.* H.M. Advocate, 1978 J.C. 70 6

Ogg *v.* H.M. Advocate, 1938 J.C. 152 20
Oghonoghor *v.* Secretary of State for the Home Department, 1996 S.L.T. 733 45
O'Hara *v.* Central SMT Co., 1941 S.C. 363 28
— *v.* H.M. Advocate, 1948 J.C. 90 53
Oliver *v.* Hislop, 1946 J.C. 20 59
O'Kelly *v.* Trust House Forte [1984] Q.B. 90 82
O'Neill *v.* Wilson, 1983 J.C. 42 73

P *v.* H.M. Advocate, 1991 S.C.C.R. 933 21
Parr *v.* H.M. Advocate, 1991 S.L.T. 208 9
Pennycuick *v.* Lees, 1992 S.C.C.R. 160 40
Perrie *v.* H.M. Advocate, 1991 S.C.C.R. 255 27
Popi M, The [1985] 2 All E.R. 712 .... 8, 87–88
Prangnell-O'Neill *v.* Skiffington, 1984 S.L.T. 282 12

Quinn *v.* Lees, 1994 S.C.C.R. 159 74

Raghip, *The Times*, Dec. 9, 1991 56
Ralston *v.* H.M. Advocate, 1987 S.C.C.R. 467 20
Ratten *v.* R. [1971] A.C. 378 .... 26, 85
Rattray *v.* Rattray (1897) 25 R. 315 45
Rees *v.* Lowe, 1989 S.C.C.R. 664 74
R. *v.* Abbot [1955] 2 All E.R. 899 16
— *v.* Ching (1976) 63 Cr.App.R. 7 15
— *v.* Exall (1866) 4 F. & F. 922 6
— *v.* Hants County Council, ex parte Ellerton [1985] 1 W.L.R. 749 14
— *v.* Home Secretary, *ex p.* Khawaja [1984] A.C. 74 14
— *v.* Kearley [1992] 2 All E.R. 345 .... 27, 84, 85, 86
— *v.* Kilbourne [1973] A.C. 729 .... 4, 47
— *v.* King [1967] 2 Q.B. 338 4
— *v.* Kritz [1950] 1 K.B. 82 15
— *v.* Murphy [1980] Q.B. 434 57
— *v.* Osborne and Virtue [1973] Q.B. 678 31
— *v.* Stagg (1980) 2 Cr.App.R.(S.) 53, C.A. 89
— *v.* Turner [1975] Q.B. 834 .... 56, 57
— *v.* Ward [1993] 1 W.L.R. 619 56
Roberts [1990] Crim.L.R. 122 56
Robertson *v.* Watson, 1949 J.C. 73 15
Robson *v.* Robson, 1973 S.L.T. (Notes) 4 61
Roy *v.* Pairman 1958 S.C. 334 47

Salusbury-Hughes *v.* H.M. Advocate, 1987 S.C.C.R. 38 83
Sanderson *v.* McManus, 1996 S.L.T. 750 26
Sands *v.* George Waterston & Sons, 1989 S.L.T. 174 77
Scott *v.* H.M. Advocate, 1946 J.C. 90 70
— *v.* Howie, 1993 S.C.C.R. 81 41
Scottish and Universal Newspapers *v.* Gherson's Trustees, 1988 S.L.T. 109 24
Sinclair *v.* Clark, 1962 J.C. 57 18
— *v.* Macdonald, 1996 S.C.C.R. 466 53
Slane *v.* H.M. Advocate, 1984 S.C.C.R. 77 51
Slowey *v.* H.M. Advocate, 1965 S.L.T. 309 72
Smith *v.* Alexander Baird, 1993 S.C.L.R. 563 .... 78, 91
— *v.* H.M. Advocate, 1986 S.C.C.R. 135 32
— *v.* Lees, 1997 S.L.T. 690 .... 17, 18
Sorley *v.* H.M. Advocate, 1992 S.L.T. 867 10
Stephen *v.* Scottish Boatowners Mutual Insurance Association, 1989 S.L.T. 283 55
Stewart *v.* H.M. Advocate, 1980 S.L.T. 245 70
Stirling Aquatic Technology *v.* Farmocean AB (No. 2), 1996 S.L.T. 456 24
Stobo *v.* H.M. Advocate, 1994 S.L.T. 28 17
Strathern *v.* Sloan, 1937 J.C. 76 61
Subramaniam *v.* Public Prosecutor [1956] 1 W.L.R. 965 .... 25, 27

Tees *v.* H.M. Advocate, 1994 S.L.T. 701 69
Templeton *v.* McLeod, 1985 S.C.C.R. 357 53
Teper *v.* R. [1952] A.C. 480 .... 25, 28, 85
Thomas *v.* Thomas, 1947 S.C. (H.L.) 45 .... 8, 81
Thomson *v.* H.M. Advocate, 1989 S.L.T. 170 42
— *v.* Tough Ropes, 1978 S.L.T. (Notes) 5 77
Todd *v.* H.M. Advocate, 1984 J.C. 13 .... 70, 71
Tonge *v.* H.M. Advocate, 1982 S.L.T. 506 .... 40, 41
Townsley *v.* Lees, 1996 S.C.C.R. 620 22
Tudhope *v.* Cullen, 1982 S.C.C.R. 276 61
— *v.* Hazleton, 1984 S.C.C.R. 455 .... 20, 21

Valentine *v.* Macphail, 1986 S.C.C.R. 321 60

W.P. *v.* Tayside Regional Council, 1989 S.C.L.R. 165 .... 62, 67
Wallace *v.* H.M. Advocate, 1952 J.C. 78 72
Walsh *v.* H.M. Advocate, 1961 J.C. 51 61
— *v.* Macphail, 1978 S.L.T. (Notes) 29 .... 36, 37
— *v.* Upper Clyde Shipbuilders, 1973 S.L.T. 182 77
Webley *v.* Ritchie, 1997 S.C.C.R. 472 37
Weightman [1991] Crim.L.R. 204 56
Weir *v.* Jessop (No. 2), 1991 S.C.C.R. 636 .... 37, 43, 89
White *v.* H.M. Advocate, 1986 S.C.C.R. 224 57
— *v.* White, 1947 S.L.T. (Notes) 51 73
Whyte *v.* Whyte (1884) 11 R. 712 47
— *v.* — (1895) 23 R. 320 61
Williamson *v.* Wither, 1981 S.C.C.R. 214 16
Wilson *v.* Brown, 1996 S.C.C.R. 470 33
— *v.* H.M. Advocate, 1987 S.C.C.R. 217 .... 19, 90
— *v.* —, 1988 S.C.C.R. 384 57
Woodhouse *v.* Hall (1980) 72 Crim.App.R. 39 27
Woodlands *v.* Hamilton, 1990 S.C.C.R. 166 19

Yates *v.* H.M. Advocate, 1977 S.L.T. (Notes) 42 18
Young *v.* Mitchell (1874) L.R. 1011 70
— *v.* NCB, 1957 S.L.T. 266 65

1. INTRODUCTION

THE LAW OF EVIDENCE

Evidence is information which tends to prove the existence of a particular fact or set of facts. The techniques used to marshal evidence and to argue about facts are common to many disciplines, including history and theology, as well as law. However, in deciding whether particular past events took place, it is very rarely possible to do so with absolute certainty. Accordingly, "proof" in law is rarely akin to proof in mathematics, where it can usually be demonstrated that the conclusion is an inevitable result of the premises applied. Instead, a court can generally draw inferences from the evidence only on the basis of greater or lesser degrees of probability. Accordingly, theories about the nature of proof and probability involve consideration of such diverse disciplines as psychology, logic, statistics, and probability theory. This must be contrasted with the *law* of evidence, which takes for granted the possibility of proof, and to some extent its nature. The legal rules concentrate instead on the means which may competently be used to prove the facts in issue between the parties to a criminal or civil case.

TERMINOLOGY

The facts in issue
The invocation of any legal rule and the granting of every legal remedy require proof of certain facts. These facts are derived by applying the substantive law to the facts of the particular case. They are known as the facts in issue, and must be averred by the party seeking the remedy in order to plead a relevant case. A failure to prove any one of these facts, such as loss or injury in a reparation case, will be fatal. The precise nature of the facts in issue will vary depending upon the type of case under consideration. In a criminal case, for example, the facts in issue will always include the fact that the crime was committed, and that it was the accused who committed it. Again, in a case based on medical negligence, the pursuer will have to establish that the treatment actually administered fell below the standard to be expected of a reasonably competent doctor, and that the breach of duty caused the injury to the pursuer. The facts in issue are variously referred to as the essential facts, the *facta probanda*, the crucial facts, or the material facts.

Evidential or circumstantial facts, or *facta probationis*
Evidential facts are facts which are not themselves in issue, but are incidental to those issues and from which inferences may be drawn about the facts in issue. Accordingly, failure to establish an evidential fact will not necessarily be fatal to proof of the case as a whole. Whether or not inferences may properly be drawn from such facts depends on the concept of relevance.

The distinction between facts in issue and evidential facts is also important for the doctrine of corroboration, which is considered in Chapter 6.

Procedural facts
A category of fact unique to criminal cases has also been identified—that of the procedural or incidental fact. These are facts about matters of procedure—for example, whether the statutory procedures for arresting a suspect in a road traffic case have been observed. They are not facts which are "in issue" in the technical sense described above, but are nevertheless facts which it is essential for the prosecutor to prove. The distinction, as Wilkinson pithily puts it, is "not altogether satisfactory".

Direct and circumstantial evidence
Broadly, direct evidence is evidence "which requires no mental process on the part of the [court] in order to draw the conclusion sought by the proponent of the evidence, other than acceptance of the evidence itself" (P. Murphy, *Evidence* (6th ed., 1997)). An eyewitness account of an event is the main example of this type of evidence. Circumstantial evidence is evidence which proves or tends to prove an evidential (or circumstantial) fact. Its significance lies in the inferences which may be drawn from it about the existence or non-existence of the facts in issue. The use of circumstantial evidence is considered further in Chapter 2.

Primary and secondary evidence
Underlying much of the law of evidence is the notion that certain— primary—types of evidence are preferable to others, which are secondary. For example, where it is alleged that a certain item is or was defective, that item should be produced as evidence, rather than a photograph or sketch of the item. This is known as the "best evidence rule". Hearsay evidence is also said to be secondary, the primary and best evidence of an event or state of affairs being that of the original witness, giving a first-hand account in court.

Testimonial, documentary and real evidence
These terms are largely self-explanatory. Testimonial or parole evidence is that given orally by a witness in court. Real evidence is that afforded by the production of any item other than a document. Documents and items of real evidence must generally be accompanied ("spoken to") by oral evidence from a witness with first-hand knowledge of the item. Following the abolition in civil cases of the rule against hearsay, however, that rule is no longer insisted upon and the use of affidavit evidence is becoming increasingly common.

Fact and opinion evidence
Witnesses are generally asked for a factual account of an event or state of affairs. In certain circumstances they may be permitted to give an opinion as to the inference which may be drawn from the facts. The most common situation in which opinion evidence is given is where the witness possesses

a particular expertise, and can assist the court in the interpretation of scientific or technical evidence.

EVIDENCE AND PROCEDURE

The laws of evidence and procedure overlap and are to some extent interdependent. For example, in both civil and criminal cases, the parties may agree certain facts, thus rendering evidence redundant. Again, in civil cases, evidence may generally be led only of matters which appear in the written pleadings (see the differing views expressed by the House of Lords on this rule in *Gibson v. BICC* (1973)). In criminal cases, the admissibility of incriminating statements by the accused may depend on the stage in the investigative process which has been reached.

CIVIL AND CRIMINAL EVIDENCE

The Scottish Law Commission has stated as a guiding principle that "the rules of the law of evidence in civil and criminal proceedings should be identical unless there is good reason to the contrary" (Scot. Law Com. Memo. No. 46, para. A.03). In a later document, however, the Commission acknowledged that there may be good reason to apply stricter evidential standards to criminal cases than to civil ones (Scot. Law Com. Report No. 149, 1995), and in fact there are now significant differences between the rules applying to the two different forms of procedure. Accordingly, a separate section (Chapter 9) will be devoted to some of the specialties of civil evidence, and in particular to the important provisions of the Civil Evidence (Scotland) Act 1988.

General reading:
T. Anderson and W. Twining, *Analysis of Evidence* (Weidenfeld and Nicholson, 1991).
A.N. Brown, *Criminal Evidence and Procedure: An Introduction* (T & T Clark, 1996).
Cohen, *The Probable and the Provable* (Oxford University Press, 1977).
Cross and Tapper, *Evidence* (8th ed., Butterworths, 1995).
Dickson, *Evidence* (3rd ed., 1887).
R. Egglestone, *Evidence, Probability and Proof* (2nd ed., Weidenfeld and Nicholson, 1983).
D. Field and F. Raitt, *The Law of Evidence in Scotland* (2nd ed., W. Green, 1996).
I.D. Macphail, *Evidence* (Law Society of Scotland, 1987).
I.D. Macphail and L.M. Ruxton, *Evidence* in The Laws of Scotland: Stair Memorial Encyclopaedia (Butterworths, 1990), Vol. 10.
P. Murphy, *A Practical Approach to Evidence* (4th ed., Blackstone, 1992).
Renton and Brown, *Criminal Procedure* (6th ed., 1996).
D.H. Sheldon, *Evidence: Cases and Materials* (W. Green, 1996).
Spencer and Flin, *The Evidence of Children* (2nd ed., Blackstone, 1993).
M. Stone, *Proof of Fact in Criminal Trials* (W. Green, 1984).
W. Twining, *Rethinking Evidence* (Northwestern University Press, 1991).
W. Twining, *Theories of Evidence* (Weidenfeld and Nicholson, 1985).

A.G. Walker and N.M.L. Walker, *The Law of Evidence in Scotland* (W. Green, 1964) (4th impression 1983).
W.A. Wilson, *Introductory Essays on Scots Law* (2nd ed., W. Green, 1984), pp. 53–62.

---

2. RELEVANCE

General
The most fundamental requirement of the law of evidence is that evidence offered in proof of an issue must be relevant to that issue. Relevance is a necessary condition of admissibility, but it is not a sufficient one. Thus, evidence which is relevant may nevertheless be excluded because of some other evidential rule. In criminal cases, for example, evidence which has been unfairly or improperly obtained is generally inadmissible however relevant or convincing it may be. The concept of relevance is not one which has been extensively analysed in Scots law (although see the recent example of *McAllister v. Normand* (1996)). Broadly, evidence is relevant if it renders more or less probable any one or more of the facts in issue. Whether evidence has this effect is in practice largely a question of "common sense" or experience (see *R. v. Kilbourne* (1973)). Experience of life tells us that the occurrence of certain events, or the presence of certain facts, is often linked or associated with other events or facts. In a divorce case in which adultery is alleged, evidence which showed that the defender spent the night in a hotel room with the alleged paramour under the name of "Mr and Mrs Smith" would probably be regarded as relevant. The inference of sexual misconduct is not irresistible, but most people would accept that it can legitimately be drawn. In other cases, the "common sense" premises on which inferences about the issues are based, arise essentially from bias or prejudice. Decisions on relevance should be carefully scrutinised for this reason. The problem has been particularly acute in relation to evidence of sexual character. In England, until relatively recently, it was considered automatically to be relevant to know that a man accused of sexual offences against young males was a homosexual (*R. v. King* (1967)). The premise on which such reasoning is based may be translated as "most homosexuals are paedophiles". Moreover, it may be that some courts and some practitioners still take the view that the sexual character of the complainer in a case of sexual assault is relevant to the question of consent (see Brown, Burman and Jamieson, *Sex Crimes on Trial* (Edinburgh, 1993) and Chapter 7 (IV)).

Fact and law
Strictly speaking, the question of relevance is one of law. It is the judge who must decide whether *any* legitimate inference can be drawn from the evidence adduced. Questions as to the strength or weight of the inferences which may be drawn from evidence are matters for the finder of fact, whether the judge or the jury. In certain cases, however, it may be difficult to

distinguish between questions of relevance and questions of weight. Evidence may be relevant in the sense that it renders a fact in issue marginally more probable. But if it yields only a weak inference about that fact because of its peripheral or marginal value, then in certain circumstances, the question becomes one of law once more. This brings us to the idea of "collateral evidence".

Collateral evidence and remoteness in relevance

While evidence may be technically relevant, its relevance may be so remote to an issue that its admission would not be justified. For example, evidence is generally excluded which is "collateral" or peripheral to the issues under consideration. Collateral evidence—sometimes also described as "similar fact evidence"—usually takes the form of evidence as to events other than the incident in question. Sometimes, however, previous events may form a sufficiently coherent pattern with the event in dispute as to render the "collateral" evidence relevant. In *W. Alexander & Sons v. Dundee Corporation* (1950), evidence was admitted of previous accidents which had occurred at the same location as that suffered by the pursuer's vehicle. The pattern of incidents was said in this case to render more likely the pursuer's contention that the road at that particular location was in an unsafe condition. Evidence of a person's character may also be excluded as being collateral or irrelevant to the matters under consideration. An additional or underlying *rationale* for this exclusion may be that the prejudicial effect of such evidence is considered to outweigh its relevance or probative value. The subject of collateral evidence is considered further in Chapter 7.

Relevance, admissibility and prejudice

Relevant evidence may be excluded from the court's consideration because of the existence of specific exclusionary rules. The basis for this is, in many cases, the idea that certain types of evidence are likely to prejudice unduly the finder of fact. Thus, it is generally not permitted to lead evidence of an accused person's previous convictions (Criminal Procedure (Scotland) Act 1995, s.101). This rule may be based either on the notion that what an accused has done on a previous occasion is irrelevant to a currently outstanding criminal charge, or on the idea that while such evidence may be to some extent relevant, it should be excluded because a jury may think it more relevant or persuasive than in fact it is.

CIRCUMSTANTIAL EVIDENCE

The relevance of direct evidence will usually be obvious. An eyewitness account of an assault in which the witness positively identifies the accused as the assailant clearly has a direct bearing on the charge against the accused. Evidence of the circumstances surrounding an alleged assault—such as bloodstains found on the accused's clothing—may not have such a clear connection to the event. Proof of the charge will therefore be dependent upon the strength and nature of the inferences which the court is prepared to draw from such evidence. Circumstantial evidence is not necessarily inferior to direct evidence, however, and it is perfectly possible to prove a case on the basis of circumstantial evidence alone. In the case of *Langan v. H.M. Advocate* (1989), for example, the only substantial evidence against the accused was that his fingerprint was found in a bloodstain at the scene of the crime. More usually, there will be a number of separate items of circumstantial evidence which, taken together, build up a picture of what took place. It is not necessary that each item of circumstantial evidence should "point" to the particular fact in issue. It is enough that the circumstances taken as a whole infer the existence of the issues concerned (*Little v. H.M. Advocate* (1983)). In the case of *Norval v. H.M. Advocate* (1978), the High Court referred to the idea of a chain of circumstantial evidence leading or pointing to the accused's guilt. It is thought, however, that a preferable analogy is that of a cable or rope, the separate strands of which represent the items of evidence in the case (see *R. v. Exall* (1866)). Unlike a chain, which will fail if one link in the chain fails, the cable is not wholly dependent upon each individual strand. If one strand fails, the cable—made up of a number of evidential or circumstantial facts—may still be able to support the weight of the case. In spite of the use of the chain analogy in *Norval*, it is clear that the High Court did not consider that the absence of one or more of the facts in the "chain" would have affected the outcome of the case. The various items of circumstantial evidence taken together yielded a strong enough inference of guilt to support the conviction. By contrast, proof of the facts in issue corresponds closely to the chain analogy. Each fact in issue, or chain-link, is essential to the case. Failure to prove a fact in issue (whether by means of direct or circumstantial evidence) is equivalent to a broken link in a chain, and, as a consequence, the case must inevitably fail. A failure to distinguish between these two concepts appears to have led the court into error in the well-known case of *Gillespie v. Macmillan* (1957), considered further in Chapter 6.

Further reading:
D.H. Sheldon, *Evidence: Cases and Materials* (W. Green, 1996), Chap. 1.
D.N. MacCormack, *Legal Reasoning and Legal Theory* (Clarendon Press, 1978).
T. Anderson and W. Twining, *Analysis of Evidence* (Weidenfeld and Nicholson, 1991), Chap. 1.
W.A. Wilson, "The Logic of Corroboration" (1960) S.L.R. 101.

---

3. THE BURDEN OF PROOF

The burden of proof on the pursuer
The incidence of the onus or burden of proof is not strictly part of the law of evidence at all, but is rather a product of the substantive law. As noted in the previous section, there are a number of elements in every court action which must be proved in order for the case to succeed. These are the facts

in issue. A pursuer in an action of reparation for personal injury, for example, must show that the defender owed him a duty of care, that that duty was breached, and that the breach caused the injury and loss of which he is complaining. By raising the action, the pursuer puts those facts in issue, and accordingly must accept the onus of proving those facts to the required standard (see *Dickinson v. Minister of Pensions* (1953)). Failure by a pursuer to discharge the onus in relation to any of the facts in issue will lead to failure in the case. It is not only the pursuer who may require to prove certain issues, however.

The burden of proof on the defender
The person who asserts a particular state of facts must, in general, prove it. A civil action proceeds in Scotland largely by way of written pleadings. These contain specific statements or averments of the facts on which each party relies. In a reparation case, a pursuer will make averments that she suffered loss, injury and damage because of the defender's negligent conduct and consequent breach of a duty of care. By making such averments, the pursuer undertakes the onus of proving them. Equally, by raising specific defences such as *volenti non fit injuria*, or contributory negligence, a defender puts those matters in issue and must prove them if the defences are to succeed. In the case of *Joseph Constantine Steamship Line Ltd v. Imperial Smelting Corporation Ltd* (1942), for example, the questions were, first, whether a charterparty had been frustrated by an explosion which sank the appellants' ship, and secondly, whether that explosion had been caused by negligence on the part of the appellants, in which case they would be unable to escape liability under the contract, whether the contract had been frustrated or not. It was held that while it was up to the appellants to prove that the contract had been frustrated, they did not bear the additional burden of proving that they had not been negligent. Rather it was for the respondents to prove the positive proposition that the appellants *had* been negligent. Thus, the burden or burdens of proof may be shared between the parties to a case, depending upon the issues raised in the pleadings.

Proof of a negative
The *Joseph Constantine* case, above, also illustrates that a party will not usually be allocated the burden of proving a negative proposition. For a defender to prove that she has performed her duties at all times with adequate skill and care, would be considerably more difficult than for the pursuer to prove that she was negligent on a particular occasion. This does not mean, however, that the onus of proof cannot lie upon a party who makes a negative allegation. If that were to be the case, then the allocation of the burden could be determined merely by manipulating the language in which a case is presented. For example, in a claim for reparation, there may be averments that the defender did not perform his duties adequately, or that he performed them negligently, but the legal or persuasive burden of establishing breach of duty is borne by the pursuer, however the claim is expressed.

In some circumstances, however, the law imposes upon parties the burden of proving a negative, usually because of some overriding practical interest or consideration of policy. In *Nimmo v. Alexander Cowan and Son Ltd* (1967), for example, an injured employee sued his employers for breach of the duty imposed by section 29 of the Factories Act 1961, which provides that every workplace shall, so far as reasonably practicable, be made and kept safe. It was held by the House of Lords that the pursuer had to show only that his workplace was not kept safe, and that the onus then rested upon his employers to show that it would not have been reasonably practicable to make the workplace any safer than it was. The decision appears to have been based largely on the consideration that the practicability of further precautions was a matter falling within the knowledge of the employer, and not the worker. It would be against the policy of the legislation, said the House of Lords, to oblige an injured worker to discharge such a burden of proof.

There is an extensive, and somewhat contradictory jurisprudence as to whether the wording of a particular statutory duty or offence requires a pursuer or prosecutor to prove all of the elements referred to in the statute, or whether the statute provides a defence—an "exception, exemption, proviso, excuse or qualification"—which must be established by the defence or the defender. For example, in *Earnshaw v. H.M. Advocate* (1981), it was held that that where the Road Traffic Act 1972, s.9(3) created the offence of "failure without reasonable excuse" to provide a laboratory specimen of blood, breath or urine, the onus of proving all the elements of this offence rests throughout on the Crown; in *Buchanan v. Price* (1982), on the other hand, it was held that where a parent is charged with an offence under the Education (Scotland) Act 1980, s.35(1) his or her child having failed "without reasonable excuse to attend regularly" at school, the burden of proving that there was a "reasonable excuse" for the failure rests on the parent. Again, what is at issue here is not strictly part of the law of evidence at all, but rather an application of the principles relating to statutory interpretation, shot through in many cases with strong policy considerations.

The effect of the burden

It should be noted that while the defender may bear the onus of proof on certain issues, failure by the defender to discharge such a burden does not necessarily mean that the pursuer will succeed. The pursuer must still prove the facts in issue to the required standard (in civil cases, on a balance of probabilities), and if the court is left unconvinced or undecided, the effect of the onus of proof lying upon the pursuer is that her action cannot succeed (*Thomas v. Thomas* (1947)). This "residual" effect is sometimes known as the *ultimate burden*. In *The Popi M* (1985), an action for recovery of insurance money, the plaintiffs had to prove that their ship had been lost through the perils of the sea. The defendants claimed that the ship was lost simply because it was unseaworthy, in which case the insurance policy was void. The plaintiffs put forward a number of hypotheses to explain the loss, including collision with a submerged rock, with an unarmed torpedo, and with a submerged submarine travelling in the same direction and at roughly the same speed as the ship. The only explanation which was not positively excluded by the evidence was that involving the submarine, an explanation which the trial judge himself admitted was "highly improbable". As the only remaining explanation, however, the trial judge felt constrained to accept it and to find for the plaintiffs. On appeal his decision was reversed. The Court of Appeal pointed out that Sherlock Holmes' famous dictum—"eliminate the impossible and whatever remains, however improbable, must be the truth"—has very limited application in the legal process. The trial judge in this case failed to appreciate that there was another option open to him—simply to find that the plaintiffs had failed to prove their case. If the submarine theory was highly improbable, it could hardly be said that the case had been proved on a balance of probabilities. Accordingly, the plaintiffs case failed, since they had failed to discharge their persuasive burden of proof.

The "shifting" burden

It is sometimes said that the burden of proof "shifts" between the parties during the course of a proof (see, *e.g. Gibson v. NCR* (1925)), as a result of one party or another leading persuasive evidence of a fact in issue. Such statements are misleading unless understood in their proper context. The onus of proving the facts in issue is usually allocated and "fixed" at the start of the case. Through their written pleadings, the parties set out the issues which they regard as crucial to their respective cases, and undertake the burden of proving those issues. The burden—sometimes called the "persuasive" or "legal" burden—of proving or disproving each issue is not transferred to the other party according to the amount and strength of evidence led. As noted above, if the court is left in doubt as to whether an issue has been established to the required standard, the party's case will fail on that issue, and may well fail in the case overall.

Tactical and evidential burdens

However, where a party has led convincing evidence on a particular issue, the other party will be well advised to lead *some* evidence on that issue, or run the risk of losing on that point. This is not to say that the latter party must positively disprove the point at issue; simply that she must lead sufficient evidence in rebuttal to tip the balance of probabilities back in her favour (or in a criminal case, to raise a reasonable doubt in the mind of the court). At the end of the case, the question for the court remains, "Has the pursuer discharged the persuasive burden on that point?" In this context, the burden of proof is sometimes called the "tactical" or "provisional" burden, and can be distinguished from the persuasive burden because it arises not through the operation of the substantive law, but from the state of the evidence (see Lord Denning's opinion in *Brown v. Rolls Royce* (1960)).

A third type of burden has been identified—the evidential burden. This is the burden of adducing enough evidence on a particular point to allow the court at least to consider the matter. This tends to have most significance in criminal cases where the accused, usually through his representatives, puts forward some defence or exculpatory argument, but leads no evidence to back it up. In such cases, the judge may well withdraw the purported defence from the jury, on the basis that there is nothing in the evidence for them to consider in relation to that defence (see, *e.g. Parr v. H.M. Advocate* (1991)).

The burden of proof in criminal cases

It is rare for the law to impose a persuasive burden on an accused person in relation to any issue. The only common law defences in relation to which the accused bears such a burden are the related ones of insanity and diminished responsibility (*Lambie v. H.M. Advocate* (1973)). There are various statutory defences which require the accused to bring himself within the exception, and such provisions may well impose a persuasive burden. In such cases, however, the accused must reach only the civil standard of proof, and need not lead corroborated evidence in support of the defence (*King v. Lees* (1993)). There may, however, be a strong evidential burden to be satisfied in relation to certain other defences. For example, it has been made clear that convincing medical evidence will have to be led in relation to a defence of automatism, even although the accused does not a bear a persuasive burden in relation to that defence (*Sorley v. H.M. Advocate* (1992)).

Further reading:

T. Denning, "Presumptions and Burdens", (1945) 61 L.Q.R. 379.
G.H. Gordon, "The Burden of Proof on the Accused", 1968 S.L.T. (News) 29, 37.
D.H. Sheldon, "Hip Flasks and Burdens", 1993 S.L.T. (News) 33.

---

4. PRESUMPTIONS

Presumptions and burdens

There is a strong link in the law between presumptions and the burden of proof. The two concepts may to some extent be considered as forming opposite sides of the same coin, for where there is a presumption there is usually a correlative burden of proof. Indeed, in some cases, the connection is even closer than this. The "presumption of innocence", for example, is simply another way of expressing the general rule that the burden of proof in a criminal case lies on the prosecution. The anomalous position of the insanity defence, which must be proved by the accused on a balance of probabilities, is a reflection of the law's general presumption of sanity. Again, the maxim *semper praesumuntur pro negante*—the presumption is always in favour of the party denying—expresses in the language of presumptions the idea that the burden in a civil case usually lies on the party asserting the truth of some proposition. As with burdens of proof, however, care must be taken in distinguishing different types of presumption.

Presumptions of law and presumptions of fact

A presumption "is an inference as to the existence of one fact, drawn from the existence of another fact". Once certain facts have been established, certain other facts will be presumed by the court. Parties can therefore use such presumptions in the discharge of their burdens of proof. They may also *create* burdens for the party against whom the presumption operates. In the same way that there may be provisional or tactical burdens, there may also be provisional presumptions—that is, a presumption which may be rebutted by leading contrary evidence. But one must distinguish between presumptions which can be rebutted only by proving the contrary position to some formal standard, and those presumptions which arise merely as a result of the state of the evidence and which may be rebutted simply by providing some credible explanation for the evidence proffered. This is the crux of the difference between presumptions of law and presumptions of fact. Presumptions of law therefore "represent what are probably the only occasions on which the legal [or persuasive] onus can properly be said to shift from one party to another" (Wilkinson, *The Scottish Law of Evidence* (1986), pp.194–195).

Conclusive "presumptions"

Some presumptions of law cannot be rebutted by the leading of evidence to any standard. Indeed the leading of such evidence is incompetent. It is, of course, self-contradictory to talk of a conclusive presumption, and in effect these "presumptions" are simply rules of law. For example, it is "conclusively presumed" that a girl under the age of 12 cannot consent to sexual intercourse; again, it is "conclusively presumed" that a child under the age of eight cannot form the *mens rea* necessary for the commission of a crime.

Activating a presumption

Presumptions do not usually render evidence wholly unnecessary. In general they do not have an independent existence, and must be "triggered" by proof of certain facts. For example, once it is shown that a person has not been known to be alive for a period of seven years, that person will be presumed to have died (Presumption of Death (Scotland) Act 1977, s.2). Again, if it is proved that a person was found in possession of recently stolen goods, and the circumstances of that possession are shown to be incriminating, then it will be presumed that that person stole the goods. These "trigger facts", and the presumptions which arise from them, may be the result of common-law development or statutory intervention. "In many cases they have little more to recommend them than practical convenience, public policy or long usage, and in some cases they fail to reflect modern attitudes and practices" (Field and Raitt, *Evidence* (2nd ed., 1996), para. 3–05).

It should be noted, however, that certain "presumptions" exist independently of any "trigger" fact. The so-called presumption of innocence, for example, may be regarded simply as a rule of law about the allocation of the burden of proof; the same is true about the presumption of sanity, referred to above. The examples given below are of the "standard" type of presumption; they require to be "activated" by the leading of evidence before coming into effect.

Presumptions of law—examples

- *Presumption of Death (Scotland) Act 1977, s.2* Where a person is thought to have died or has not been known to be alive for a period of seven years, then it is presumed that he or she has died, unless the contrary is proved.

- *Succession (Scotland) Act 1964, s.31* Where two persons die in circumstances which indicate that they died simultaneously or which render it uncertain which of them died first, then, subject to exceptions, it is presumed that the younger survived the elder. However, the presumption operates only where there is no proof of survivorship (*Lamb v. Lord Advocate* (1976)).
- *Child-bearing and begetting* It is presumed that women beyond a certain age are incapable of child-bearing, unless, of course, the contrary can be proved (*G's Trustees v. G* (1936)). There is no such presumption in relation to the begetting of children by men.
- *Illegitimacy* It is presumed that where a married woman gives birth, the child's father is her husband, thus rendering the child legitimate (*Pater est qui nuptiae demonstrant*). This presumption can be rebutted on a balance of probabilities (Law Reform (Parent and Child)(Scotland) Act 1986, s.5). Formerly, the presumption was regarded as a very strong one and required rebuttal beyond reasonable doubt (*Imre v. Mitchell* (1958)).
- *Regularity and validity* Documents and other official materials or procedures are presumed to be valid in substance if they are valid on their face. Thus, in *Edinburgh District Council v. MacDonald* (1979), where it was claimed that a statutory notice had not been received, the fact that the usual office procedures were shown to have been followed by the local authority was enough to trigger a presumption that the notice had in fact been sent out, a presumption which could not, in the event, be rebutted.
- *Presumption of ownership arising from the possession of moveables* This presumption is often classifed as one of fact (see *Prangnell-O'Neill v. Skiffington* (1984)). But it is clear that in order to rebut the presumption, the pursuer must prove that she once owned the article concerned, and that her possession came to an end in such a way that the new possessor could not have become the owner. The requirement for proof of these matters suggests a presumption of law rather than a provisional presumption or presumption of fact.

Presumptions of fact—examples

- *The "doctrine" of recent possession* Where a person is found in possession of goods which have been recently stolen, and the circumstances of that possession are incriminating, then it is presumed that the possessor is the thief. Some of the case law suggests that this presumption is one of law (*e.g. Fox v. Patterson* (1948)). This view has been criticised, notably by Sheriff Gordon, and it seems to have been accepted that the presumption is a provisional one only (*Macdonald v. H.M. Advocate* (1989)).

• *Res ipsa loquitur* This is the idea that where, in a reparation action, an accident is proved to have been caused by a thing which was within the control or management of the defender, and the accident was such as would not have happened in the ordinary course of things if those with managerial control had exercised proper care, then it is presumed that the accident was caused by the defender's negligence. In the normal case, however, this presumption can be rebutted provided that it is established that conditions were present which might have caused the accident without negligence on the part of the defender. Where the accident comes about as a result of "voluntary human action" then the presumption of negligence is a stronger one, and apparently transfers a persuasive burden of proof on to the defender (*Devine v. Colvilles* (1969)).

Further reading:
T. Denning,"Presumptions and Burdens" (1945) 61 L.Q.R. 379.
G.H. Gordon, "The Burden of Proof on the Accused", 1968 S.L.T. (News) 29, 37.
Field and Raitt, *Evidence* (W. Green, 1996), Chap. 3.

---

5. THE STANDARD OF PROOF

THE NATURE OF PROOF

The nature of "legal probability" is controversial, but it certainly seems to be unlike mathematical or "Pascalian" probability. It is rarely possible to demonstrate that an accused person committed an offence with the same degree of certainty by which it is possible to demonstrate the truth of Pythagoras' theorem, for example. Instead, what is required is evidence sufficient to instil in the court the requisite degree of belief or conviction as to the facts in issue. This degree of belief has been described as "subjective probability". Given an infinite variety of fact-situations and the presence of so many subjective variables in the fact-finding process, it is difficult or impossible to express the appropriate standard of subjective probability in anything other than very general, common-sense terms.

Faced with the practical problem that decisions must be made in imperfect conditions, the courts will usually accept evidence which falls short of certainty (although compare *Imre v. Mitchell* (1958)). The nature and amount of evidence which brings home conviction to the mind of the court will inevitably vary from case to case. Once the court is convinced to the appropriate standard, however, the issue is regarded as "proved", even although there may remain a degree of uncertainty about that issue. Thus, "in determining what did happen in the past a court decides on the balance of probabilities. Anything that is more probable than not it treats as certain" (Lord Diplock in *Mallett v. McMonagle* (1970)). What is regarded as the "appropriate standard", however, may differ depending upon the nature of the proceedings.

CIVIL CASES

The basic rule
The standard of proof in civil cases has been expressed as a balance of probabilities *Hendry v. Clan Line Steamers* (1949)). A fact is said to be proved if it can be shown to be more probable than not. This will be so even if there is a substantial probability—theoretically as much as 49 per cent—in favour of the other party. It is here that the distinction between civil and criminal cases is at its clearest, since any real probability in favour of an accused person should lead to an acquittal.

Intermediate standards?
It has sometimes been suggested that there may, in civil cases, be a standard of proof higher than the normal civil standard, but lower than the criminal standard (see, *e.g. Lennon v. Co-operative Insurance Society* (1985)). Such suggestions have been firmly rejected in Scotland, even in respect of cases involving allegations of serious crime. There are only two standards of proof—proof on a balance of probabilities and proof beyond reasonable doubt (*B v. Kennedy* (1987); *Mullan v. Anderson* (1993)). More subtly, it has been suggested that the civil standard is a flexible or variable one (*Bater v. Bater* (1951)) and that, in civil cases, the more serious the allegation, the higher the degree of probability which is required to establish that allegation (see *inter alia* the English cases of *R. v. Home Secretary, ex parte Khawaja* (1984) and *R. v. Hants County Council, ex parte Ellerton* (1985)). This point has not yet been authoritatively settled in Scots law—there are dicta in *Harris v. F* (1991) which suggest that the standards are fixed, while in *Mullan v. Anderson* (1993) some members of the court appear to take the opposite view. There is much force in the argument that the more serious the allegation, the greater should be the weight of evidence required to tip the balance of probability. However, this should not be taken to mean that in some cases a probability of (say) 75 per cent is required, while in others 51 per cent will suffice. If a fact is more probable than not then, in a civil case, it is deemed to be established.

Quasi-criminal matters
Issues may occasionally arise in civil cases which, if proved, may lead to the imposition of financial penalties or even imprisonment. The most obvious example is contempt of court. Failure to observe or obtemper any order of the court may constitute a contempt, and may be punished by the court without recourse to the criminal courts. In such cases, however, it has been held that the standard of proof is the criminal standard, given the serious consequences of a finding of contempt (see, *e.g. Johnston v. Johnston* (1996)). The same approach is taken in all cases in which some question of quasi-criminal penalties may arise. Thus, cases involving the imposition of

penalties for failure to pay tax or failure to obtemper decrees *ad factum praestandum* or for interdict all seem to require proof beyond reasonable doubt. There is recent authority, however, that in cases involving the imposition of a penalty for failure to pay VAT, the standard of proof is the civil standard only (*Re Indian Cavalry Club Ltd and Another* (1997)).

CRIMINAL CASES

The standard of proof in criminal cases is proof beyond a reasonable doubt. The standard does not require certainty, but does require a high degree of probability, and any doubt left in the mind of the court which is more than a "remote or fanciful possibility" must lead to the acquittal of the accused (*Miller v. Minister of Pensions* (1947)). There have occasionally been attempts to define more fully what is required by the criminal standard. But directions referring to a reasonable doubt as being "one for which you can give a reason", or "a doubt which might affect you in the conduct of your everyday affairs" and other similar formulations, have been disapproved by courts both in England and Scotland (see, *e.g. R. v. Ching* (1976); see also *R. v. Kritz* (1950)). Each of the facts in issue must be established to the criminal standard by the prosecution and, in addition, all of the facts in issue in a criminal case must be corroborated (corroboration is considered further in Chapter 6). In those rare cases—such as the insanity defence—in which a persuasive burden of proof rests on the accused, the standard is the lower civil standard (*H.M. Advocate v. Mitchell* (1951); *Robertson v. Watson* (1949)). It seems, however, that in such cases the accused may reach the required standard without leading corroborated evidence (*King v. Lees* (1993)).

Further reading:
J. Cohen, *The Probable and the Provable* (Clarendon Press, 1977).
R. Egglestone, *Evidence, Proof and Probability* (2nd ed., Weidenfeld and Nicholson, 1983), Chaps. 9 and 10.

---

6. SUFFICIENCY OF EVIDENCE

As we saw in the previous section, the evidence in either a civil or a criminal case must be such as to satisfy the court to the appropriate standard of proof. The degree to which the evidence convinces the court about the facts in issue is itself a question of fact and, as we have seen, is probably not a matter about which precise rules can be laid down, given the infinite variety of fact-situations which may arise. Behind the question of the weight to be given to the evidence, however, is the question of sufficiency. Sufficiency is a question of law, and prior to the question of weight. If there is insufficient evidence in law, then the case should be withdrawn from the fact-finder before any question as to the *quality* of the evidence can arise.

Civil cases

Prior to 1968 (and section 9 of the Law Reform (Miscellaneous Provisions) (Scotland) Act 1968), corroboration was required in all civil cases. Following the Civil Evidence (Scotland) Act 1988 it is required in none. Specialties of civil evidence, and in particular the significant changes made to the law by the 1988 Act, are considered in Chapter 9. It should be noted here, however, that the question of sufficiency does retain an importance in civil cases in spite of the fact that corroboration is not required. As we have already seen, each of the crucial facts in a case, whether criminal or civil, must be established to the appropriate standard. If a party to a civil case fails to lead evidence which establishes a crucial fact on a balance of probabilities, then her case must fail, and in that sense that party has led insufficient evidence in law.

No case to answer

The question arises most acutely in criminal cases, however, since in such cases, corroboration *is* required. On the completion of the Crown's evidence, the defence may make a submission to the court under sections 97 or 160 of the Criminal Procedure (Scotland) Act 1995 that there is no case to answer. The submission is based on the premise that if the Crown fails to produce sufficient evidence in law—that is, corroborated evidence of each of the facts in issue—the case against the accused must fail and he should be acquitted immediately. In considering the question of sufficiency at this stage, the trial judge must take the Crown case "at its highest": that is she must assume that the Crown evidence can be accepted in its entirety. If even on that assumption there is insufficient evidence in law, then the submission should succeed (*Williamson v. Wither* (1981)). If the submission is rejected then the case continues, and the defence must decide whether to lead evidence in rebuttal of the Crown's case or not. There is no obligation on the defence to do so, but if they do not, clearly there is a risk that the accused will be convicted. (This is a good illustration of the idea of the tactical burden.) The mere fact that there is sufficient evidence in law does not guarantee a conviction, however, because of the question of the weight to be ascribed to the evidence. Although technically there may be a sufficiency of evidence, that evidence may be of poor quality or lacking credibility. Accordingly, corroboration is a necessary, but not a sufficient, condition for a criminal conviction.

Difficulties may arise if a submission of no case to answer is mistakenly rejected by the trial judge, and the defence goes on to give evidence which is in fact corroborative of the Crown case. In England, there has been at least one case (*R. v. Abbot* (1955)) in which evidence given for the defence in such circumstances has been excluded, and the conviction quashed. The circumstances of *Abbot* were rather special, however, and it seems likely that in Scotland a more robust view would be taken. After all, in order to appeal successfully against a conviction it is necessary to show that there has been a miscarriage of justice, and where there is sufficient credible evidence in the case to justify conviction, it would be difficult to argue that there has been such a miscarriage, even where all of that evidence would not have been led but for the judge's error.

Corroboration—general

Corroboration is evidence which supports or confirms the effect of other testimony (*Fox v. H.M. Advocate* (1998)). Its value lies in the protection it provides against wrongful conviction as a result of a lying or mistaken witness. Its principal demerit is that it renders conviction more difficult in cases—particularly those involving sexual offences—where corroboration may be difficult to obtain.

Corroboration—the basic rule

The basic rule is that a case must be proved by evidence from at least two independent sources (Renton and Brown, *Criminal Procedure*). However, it seems to be generally accepted that in order to provide sufficient evidence in law, the prosecution must lead corroborated evidence of each of the facts in issue (*Lockwood v. Walker* (1910); *Smith v. Lees* (1997)).

There is sufficient evidence in law if two or more witnesses give direct evidence about those facts. Circumstantial evidence is also capable of corroborating direct evidence, however. There can even be sufficient evidence in law where the evidence against the accused is entirely circumstantial, provided that it comes from at least two sources. *Langan v. H.M. Advocate* (1989) provides an extreme example of this. The only evidence of any substance against the accused in that case was that his fingerprint was found in a bloodstain at the scene of the murder. The accused's denial that he was ever at the scene was disbelieved, and he was convicted. Although there was only one item of evidence in the case, it was sufficient to convict because it was spoken to by more than one witness.

Corroboration, confirmation and evidential support

At one time, it was thought to be sufficient that the corroborative evidence be "consistent" with the evidence of principal witness (see, *e.g. Stobo v. H.M. Advocate* (1994)). It has been held, however, that mere consistency is not enough. What is required is evidence which supports or confirms the case against the accused (*Fox v. H.M. Advocate* (1998)). Corroborative evidence must therefore be both consistent and incriminating, at least when taken together with the principal evidence. Conversely, evidence which is *in*consistent with the evidence of the main witness cannot provide corroboration (*McDonald v. Scott* (1993)). Where the Crown evidence is entirely circumstantial, there is no need for each separate item or adminicle of evidence to "point" to the accused's guilt. It is enough that the various circumstances taken together will support the necessary inference of guilt (*Little v. H.M. Advocate* (1983)).

SPECIAL CASES

Distress as corroboration

To alleviate the difficulty of providing corroboration in cases where the only witness to the event is the complainer, it came to be accepted that distress manifested by the complainer shortly after the alleged incident, and independently observed, could form corroboration of her own account (*Yates v. H.M. Advocate* (1977)). However, distress may have a number of causes, and it may be difficult unequivocally to refer distress to the facts in issue in a particular case. In a case of alleged rape, for example, evidence of distress cannot generally be used to show that intercourse took place, since intercourse is not an inherently distressing event. Where the rape is said to have been achieved by force, evidence of distress is again unhelpful, since the distress could easily have been caused by the physical force used, rather than by any sexual element to the incident.

The leading case is *Smith v. Lees* (1997) in which it was held that the complainer's distress could not corroborate a charge of lewd practices. The incident was said to have taken place in a tent in which the accused and the complainer were sleeping. The complainer had emerged from the tent in a slightly distressed condition, claiming that the accused had placed her hand on his penis while she was asleep. There was nothing, however, other than the complainer's own account, to show that it was that conduct which *caused* her distress, rather than something which was said by the accused, or even dreamt by the complainer. Distress therefore has a very narrow application in providing corroboration, and will be limited to cases where the relevance of distress is clear. In practice this may mean only those cases in which the complainer's state of mind is in issue (*Smith v. Lees*, above). The most common situation in which this is likely to arise is where, on a charge of rape, intercourse is admitted and the only dispute is as to consent. In such circumstances, evidence of distress becomes highly relevant since, as noted above, consensual intercourse is not usually distressing.

Confessions

In contrast with some other jurisdictions, the fact that an accused person in Scotland has confessed extra-judicially to an offence is not conclusive against him in Scotland. Corroboration is still required (*Sinclair v. Clark* (1962)). In *Hartley v. H.M. Advocate* (1979), and some subsequent cases, however, it was suggested that where there is a clear and unequivocal confession of guilt, very little corroboration is required. This was on the basis that a confession, being prejudicial to the accused's own interests, may initially be assumed to be true. However, there is no such rule of law (*Meredith v. Lees* (1992)). What is required in each case is evidence which is capable of providing "an independent check of the guilt of the accused". The quality and strength of such evidence may vary according to the circumstances, and where a confession seems particularly trustworthy or compelling, a court *may* accept somewhat less in the way of corroboration than might otherwise be the case.

Special knowledge confessions

There is one type of confession which does not require corroboration from an independent source. This is the so-called "special knowledge" confession. Where a confession contains information which shows that the accused has "inside" or special knowledge about the offence, the confession may effectively corroborate itself. There must, of course, be independent confirmation of the information in question. However, the confession provides the only link between the information and the accused. The rule arose initially from the case of *Manuel v. H.M. Advocate* (1958). In that case the accused confessed to a number of murders. In relation to one of those killings, he gave details of the whereabouts of the murder weapon, and certain items of the victim's clothing. He subsequently led the police to these items, the latter apparently having had no prior knowledge of their location. In these circumstances, the court accepted that there was sufficient evidence against the accused in relation to this particular murder.

The decision in *Manuel* was based largely on a passage in Alison which refers to the situation in which the accused leads "the officer who seized him" to the stolen goods, the murder weapon, the victim's body, or whatever; to the situation, in other words, in which the confession reveals something which the investigating authorities did not already know, and which could have been known only to the perpetrator. In subsequent cases, however, the courts have formulated a rather less strict test in relation to special knowledge confessions. In cases such as *Wilson v. H.M. Advocate* (1987), the High Court accepted as "special knowledge" information which was already known to the authorities, and which was indeed largely public knowledge. This involved the adoption of a test which required the jury to decide whether the information was known to the accused *because* he was the perpetrator, and the rejection of the idea that the "special" knowledge was such that only the perpetrator could have possessed it. Moreover, this rule has itself been applied rather loosely. In *Gilmour v. H.M. Advocate* (1982), for example, a confession was accepted as demonstrating special knowledge, even although some of the information contained in it was inaccurate or false; and in *McDonald v. H.M. Advocate* (1987), the statement accepted as showing special knowledge was merely "I told you, I did that one with Kenny and Bruce", where there were two co-accused with those names.

Two more recent cases show, however, that there are limits to the extent to which self-corroborating confessions will be accepted—*Woodlands v. Hamilton* (1990) and *Low v. H.M. Advocate* (1993). As well as suggesting that something more substantial than "Kenny and Bruce" will be required in the way of special knowledge, the latter case also holds that where it is proposed to rely upon a special knowledge confession, that confession must be spoken to by two witnesses. This is in contrast to "ordinary" confessions, which may be proved by a single witness only, since the case against the accused is corroborated by other witnesses. In *Mitchell v. H.M. Advocate* (1996), however, it was held that it is enough if the *confession* is spoken to by two witnesses; it is not necessary that two witnesses speak to every element in the confession relied upon as demonstrating special knowledge.

Identification cases

The reasoning in *Meredith v. Lees*, above, presumably also applies to those cases (such as *Ralston v. H.M. Advocate* (1987)) in which it has been said that "where one starts with an emphatic positive identification by one witness then very little else is required". Again, the correct view must be that there is no such rule, and the strength of the corroboration required will vary according to the circumstances of each case. In the recent case of *Mair v. H.M. Advocate* (1997), it was held that where it is sought to corroborate a positive identification by a witness, then the corroborative evidence must be consistent "in all respects" with the main identification.

The "Moorov" doctrine

In many cases, especially sexual ones, which tend to take place in private, it may be difficult to satisfy the requirement for corroboration. This difficulty contributed to the development of the doctrine of mutual corroboration, in which a number of separate, but similar, offences may corroborate one another, even although only one witness speaks to each. The modern doctrine was first enunciated in the case of *Moorov v. H.M. Advocate* (1930)). In that case, the accused was charged with a series of assaults and indecent assaults against female employees, all within a period of about three years, and all of which took place while no one else was present. The court held that, provided the different incidents were shown to be so connected in relation to their time, location and mode of commission as to afford an inference of some underlying or unifying scheme or circumstance, the single witnesses to each offence could afford corroboration to one another. In *Moorov* this underlying project was said to be "a campaign of lustful indulgence at the expense of his female employees". The High Court emphasised in later cases such as *Ogg v. H.M. Advocate* (1938), that mere proof of a general disposition to commit a particular type of offence is insufficient to invoke mutual corroboration. In *Moorov* itself, Lord Justice General Clyde disapproved of the idea that proof of a course of similar conduct was sufficient. In modern practice, however, it is just such a course of conduct that the courts tend to look for, and indeed in *Tudhope v. Hazleton* (1984), Lord Justice Clerk Wheatley explicitly approved the use of this phrase as being one which "aptly focuses the important factor for the benefit of a judge or a jury".

Similarity
Mere similarity is not enough, however. In *Tudhope v. Hazleton* (1984), for example, the prosecutor listed some 12 points of similarity between the separate incidents involved. This was still not enough, in the opinion of the court, to justify invoking the doctrine. In the circumstances of this case, it was said that these were merely isolated incidents, with nothing positively to link them together in the manner required by *Moorov*.

The nature of the offences

The requirement for similarity in the circumstances surrounding the offences was taken in the past to imply that the separate charges had to libel the same offence. More recently, however, the court has accepted that the doctrine may operate provided that the offences involved are of the same type. Thus, in *Carpenter v. Hamilton* (1994), a charge of breach of the peace was held capable of corroborating one of indecent exposure where the conduct complained of in the two charges was of a similar—indecent— nature. Similarly, a charge of rape and one of sodomy were held to be mutually corroborative in *P v. H.M. Advocate* (1991) given that both involved penetrative sexual assaults.

Close connection in time

For the doctrine to operate, the charges must disclose conduct which is not only similar in nature, but which is closely connected in terms of time. A typical *Moorov* case might involve a number of charges separated by only a few days or weeks. Such a close connection in time assists the court in concluding that the separate incidents all formed part of the same "adventure" or course of conduct. However, this requirement is subject to the circumstances of the particular case. A serial bigamist will require rather more time to complete his criminal "project" than will a person who is in the habit of exposing himself indecently, or who makes a living by passing forged cheques. This is especially true in relation to sexual offences against children, where a parent or guardian may abuse a number of children in the household, when each reaches a particular age or stage of development. Thus, lengthy periods between separate charges may be permitted in some cases. In *Coffey v. Houston* (1992), an interval of two years between the incidents was accepted; in *Tudhope v. Hazleton*, on the other hand, a period of 15 months was not. It should be noted, however, that the former case involved charges of sexual abuse, and may illustrate the latitude given in the application of *Moorov* to such cases.

Identification in each case

Finally, where *Moorov* is relied upon, it was traditionally thought that there must be a positive identification of the accused in relation to each separate incident (*McRae v. H.M. Advocate* (1975)). This may be by means of circumstantial rather than direct evidence (*Lindsay v. H.M. Advocate* (1994)). However, in *Howden v. H.M. Advocate* (1994) the court held that, provided there is a positive identification in relation to one incident and evidence that the perpetrator of each incident was the same, the accused may be convicted of all the separate charges. It should be noted, however, that the court in *Howden* specifically disclaimed any attempt to apply the *Moorov* doctrine, and there is no doubt that this was not a typical *Moorov* case, since there was apparently sufficient evidence to convict of one of the two incidents charged without any recourse to the doctrine. Nevertheless, it is arguable that *Howden* represents a weakening of the doctrine, or of the corroboration requirement in general, since it uses evidence in relation to one charge partially to corroborate a fact in issue in relation to another charge. *Howden* was explicitly followed in the case of *Townsley v. Lees* (1996).

Further reading:
"Corroboration of Evidence in Scottish Criminal Law" (Contributed), 1958 S.L.T. (News) 137.
P. Ferguson, "Corroboration and Similar Fact Evidence", 1996 S.L.T. (News) 339.
G.H. Gordon, "At the Mouth of Two Witnesses" in *Justice and Crime: Essays in Honour of the Right Honourable The Lord Emslie* (R.F. Hunter ed., T&T Clark, 1993).
R. Shiels, "Corroboration by Distress" (1994) 39 J.L.S.S. 293.
W.A. Wilson, "The Logic of Corroboration", 1960 S.L.R. 101.

---

7. ADMISSIBILITY OF EVIDENCE

GENERAL

Even where evidence is relevant to a fact in issue, it may not be admissible in the proceedings because of some exclusionary rule. The rules on admissibility of evidence in Scotland have become considerably more liberal in the last few years, and Scots law generally seems to take a rather more relaxed attitude to admissibility than in some other jurisdictions, the most important consideration being relevance. Nevertheless, some significant exceptions remain. This section deals primarily with admissibility in criminal proceedings, civil matters being dealt with elsewhere.

1. THE BEST EVIDENCE RULE

The best evidence rule has been described (notably by Dickson) as the primary rule of evidence, and it is true that many of the rules of evidence have their origin in, or at least something in common with, this rule. In modern practice, however, the rule is of little significance, and its application very limited. It is sometimes said that the rule excluding hearsay is an aspect of the best evidence rule. This claim is controversial in the Scottish context, however, and in any event, the law on hearsay is now so extensive and specialised that it is treated under a separate heading.

The best evidence rule in essence forbids the use of evidence which is secondary or substitutionary in character, and demands instead original or primary evidence unless there is good reason why such evidence cannot be produced. Thus, the court would normally require an item of real evidence to be produced and spoken to, rather than photographs or oral descriptions of it, or the production of the original of a document, rather than a photocopy.

Criminal law

The rule still forms a part of the criminal law of evidence, although as noted above, not a very significant part. There is no doubt that a party ought generally to adduce the best evidence of a particular matter. But while in the past the onus appears to have been on a party failing to produce an item to provide a good reason for non-production (*Maciver v. McKenzie* (1942)), more recent cases have come close to inverting the onus, so that an item need not be produced unless it is shown that failure to do so would prejudice the other party. Thus, in *Macleod v. Woodmuir Miners Welfare Society Social Club* (1961), Lord Justice General Clyde said that: "Primary evidence is not always essential, and secondary evidence is not necessarily incompetent. Secondary evidence is competent if it is not reasonably practicable and convenient to produce the primary evidence."

In the case of *Anderson v. Laverock* (1976), the accused was charged with taking salmon by means of a gaff or cleek—an illegal method—and out of season. The fish were not produced at the trial, but the prosecution were permitted to lead oral—that is, secondary—evidence of their condition when examined after the accused's arrest. On appeal it was held that production of the fish was not necessary, since the items were obviously perishable, and it would not be practicable or convenient to produce them. The conviction was quashed, however, on the ground that the defence were not given the opportunity to examine the fish before they were destroyed, and this failure prejudiced the defence, since the condition of the fish, and in particular the presence or absence of the type of marks made by gaffs or cleeks, was clearly an important issue in the case.

More recent cases have continued to emphasise these elements of practicability, convenience, and prejudice. For example, in *McKellar v. Normand* (1992), a case in which the accused was charged with the reset of a bed and a blanket, neither the items in question, nor labels in lieu of the objects, were produced at the trial. On appeal the High Court held that there was no necessity to produce the items. In spite of the absence of any explanation by the Crown for the failure to produce them, it held further that before secondary evidence about the items would be excluded, the defence had to show that the failure to produce the items caused prejudice to the accused. Accordingly, it is enough that the court takes the view, either at first instance or on appeal, that inconvenience or difficulty would be caused by a requirement to produce the items. There is no need for a specific finding of fact to that effect (*Morrison v. Mackenzie* (1990)). In the light of these and other cases (see *McLeod v. Fraser* (1986), and *Houston v. McLeod* (1986)), it has been suggested, notably by Sheriff Gordon, that the best evidence rule is now of little importance in criminal cases.

Paradoxically, however, the best evidence rule does retain a certain formal significance. In *Deb v. Normand* (1996), it was held that a police officer could not be obliged to produce his notebook to support his oral evidence. The best evidence was constituted by his own recollection of events, and his notes were secondary (and therefore inferior in law) despite having been made at the time of the incident concerned.

Civil cases

The best evidence rule was, until 1988, applied if anything more strictly in civil cases than in criminal ones. *McGowan v. Belling* (1983), for example, was a claim for reparation for injuries sustained in a fire allegedly caused by a faulty electric heater. The case failed because of the pursuer's failure, without satisfactory explanation, to produce the remains of the heater. In *Scottish and Universal Newspapers v. Gherson's Trustees* (1988), the court said that secondary evidence regarding certain documents would not be admitted unless the party seeking to adduce the evidence gave an explanation for the failure to produce the originals which did not involve fault on their part. However, prejudice remains an important consideration. In *Stirling Aquatic Technology v. Farmocean AB (No. 2)* (1996), secondary evidence as to the condition of nets used by the pursuers at their fish farm was permitted, on the basis that they were no longer in a condition in which they could usefully be examined. Lord Johnston said that:

> "In my opinion the best evidence rule is essentially tied up with questions of prejudice in the sense that if there is better evidence than that adduced before the court, the party affected by it is prejudiced in his attack upon it and the proferring party thus gains an unfair advantage. I do not see how this rule can apply if it is no longer possible to bring the net to court in any useful state. The question of preservation raises another question. In my view the proper approach to the issue is to view the pursuer's case with considerably more care as to its quality than might otherwise be necessary if the net had been produced, or preserved for production, imposing a heavier burden of proof upon the pursuers than might otherwise have been necessary."

The best evidence rule, and the requirement enunciated in *Gherson's Trustees* remains in relation to items of real evidence (see *Stirling Aquatic Technology v. Farmocean AB (No. 2)*, above). In relation to documents, the rule has been substantially abrogated by the Civil Evidence (Scotland) Act 1988. Section 6 of that Act deems copy documents to be equivalent to originals, provided that they are authenticated "by a person responsible for the making of the copy". Two points arise from section 6:

- In the first place it is unclear exactly what is meant by "the person responsible" for making the copy. It is submitted that the person responsible is the person who instructed the copy to be made, rather than the person who actually made the copy, assuming that they are different.
- It is also unclear how section 6 fits into the general scheme of the Act. In *McIlveny v. Donald* (1995) it was held that in order to be deemed a true copy under section 6, a copy document must be authenticated *prior* to its being lodged as a production. In so far as this case implies that unauthenticated copies are wholly inadmissible, however, it is respectfully submitted that *McIlveny v. Donald* cannot be correct. Section 2 of the 1988 Act permits secondary evidence of any "statement"

provided that certain conditions are met (see the separate chapter on Civil Evidence). The definition of "statement" in section 9 of the Act includes "any representation (however made or expressed) of fact or opinion". Therefore, a statement made in a document appears to fall within the section 9 definition. By section 2, "a statement made by a person otherwise than in the course of the proof shall be admissible as evidence of any matter contained in the statement of which direct oral evidence by that person would be admissible". Accordingly, the way would seem to be clear to lead either a document itself or oral evidence about its contents if the document is not produced. While the document will not automatically be deemed equivalent to the original, it can (and, it is suggested, must) be taken into account for what it is worth.

Further reading:
Nicol, "Best Evidence in Criminal Cases", 1990 S.L.T. (News) 149

II. THE HEARSAY RULE

Hearsay is "evidence of a statement made by a person otherwise than while giving oral evidence in court". It is generally inadmissible. In the Privy Council case of *Teper v. R.* (1952), Lord Normand said that:
> "The rule against the admission of hearsay evidence is fundamental. It is not the best evidence and it is not delivered on oath. The truthfulness and accuracy of the person whose words are spoken to by another witness cannot be tested by cross-examination, and the light which his demeanour would throw on his testimony is lost. Nevertheless, the rule admits of certain carefully safeguarded and limited exceptions."

In fact the rule is probably of little importance in modern Scottish practice. It has been altogether abolished in civil cases (see the Civil Evidence (Scotland) Act 1988, s.2 and the chapter on Civil Evidence). In criminal cases there are now so many exceptions as to leave the rule itself little more than a rump. In any event, there are few reported Scottish cases on the hearsay rule, and the English cases must be read with a certain amount of caution given the differences which exist in the scope of the rule between the two jurisdictions.

Primary and secondary hearsay

There is in the first place a distinction to be made between two different ways in which hearsay evidence may be used. In *Subramaniam v. Public Prosecutor* (1956), another Privy Council case, it was said that:
> "Evidence of a statement ... is hearsay and inadmissible when the object of the evidence is to establish the truth of what is contained in the statement. It is not hearsay and is admissible when it is proposed to establish by the evidence, not the truth of the statement, but the fact that it was made".

These different types of hearsay are sometimes described respectively as secondary and primary hearsay. Hearsay is secondary and inadmissible only where it is being used "testimonially", that is as if it were the evidence of a person being given in court (see *Ratten v. R.* (1971)). Where the statement is significant in its own right, rather than for the information contained in it, it is admissible as original evidence about a fact in issue. In *McLaren v. McLeod* (1913), for example, police officers were permitted to give evidence of a statement overheard by them in a house alleged to be a brothel. The statement was made by one of the female occupants of the house to another, and was to the effect that the accused had introduced "short time" to the house. The nature or character of this statement was said to be relevant to the libel regardless of the truth or falsity of the information contained in it, and evidence about the statement was admitted as primary hearsay. In the more recent case of *McLeod v. Lowe* (1993), the question was whether the police had reasonable grounds to suspect that the accused was in possession of controlled drugs and were therefore entitled to search him. Their suspicion was said to rest on a statement made to them by members of staff at the hotel where the accused was arrested. On an appeal against his conviction the accused argued that there was no admissible evidence before the court to justify the finding that the police had reasonable grounds to suspect him of the offence. Refusing the appeal, the Court said:

> "What was at issue was the information on which the police acted. Evidence about that could competently have been given by either the hotel staff or the police officers themselves. The evidence of the police officers to this effect would not have proved the truth of what they were told by the hotel staff but it could have proved that the statements were made. In other words what the Crown were endeavouring to lead from the police witnesses was primary hearsay which was admissible as direct evidence that the statement was made irrespective of its truth or falsehood".

Hearsay is now generally admissible in civil cases (Civil Evidence (Scotland) Act 1988, s.2). In the rare instances where it is not, the rule permitting primary hearsay still applies. In *Sanderson v. McManus* (1996), for example, certain hearsay statements made by a child were held to be inadmissible as evidence of the facts asserted in them. There were, however, a number of statements, all made shortly after periods of access with the child's father, all made spontaneously, and all to the effect that the father had assaulted the child during those periods of access. The sheriff admitted the statements for the limited purpose of showing that there had been a number of complaints from the child immediately following periods of access. These complaints were held to be relevant to the question of whether or not the father should be refused access to the child. The sheriff's view was upheld on appeal all the way to the House of Lords.

Other situations in which primary hearsay statements are admissible include: the situation in which the statement forms the subject-matter of the charge (as in cases of bribery or fraud, for example); where the statement is relevant to demonstrate a state of mind such as knowledge of certain facts, or perhaps insanity; or where they are relevant to show consistency of story and hence bolster credibility—although the *de recenti* complaint appears to be the only example of this (see *Morton v. H.M. Advocate* (1938)). In general, evidence which merely supports the credibility of a witness is not admissible (see *Morrison v. H.M. Advocate* (1990), considered further below).

The creation of further exceptions to the hearsay rule

In England the courts have made it clear that the broad category of exceptions to the hearsay rule proper is closed, and that any further modification of the rule must be left to Parliament (see most recently *R. v. Kearley* (1992)). By contrast, the Scottish courts have taken a much more "liberal" attitude to development of the rule. In *Perrie v. H.M. Advocate* (1991), the High Court said that the category of exceptions to the hearsay rule was not closed, although in the circumstances declined to create a new exception (to allow the admission of incriminating statements by persons other than the accused). In *Lord Advocate's Reference (No. 1 of 1992)* (1992), a new exception was created in relation to computer records. Print-outs from a computer, of course, represent statements made by the person who created the record concerned. Unless that person could be called as a witness, evidence of the print-out would be inadmissible as hearsay. In this case, however, it was held that where it was wholly impracticable to locate and call the programmer as a witness, then the print-out became the best evidence available to the court and should be admitted as such. This idea that hearsay may become the best evidence available to a court, appears to have formed the basis for the reforms introduced by the Criminal Justice (Scotland) Act 1995, considered in detail below. Given the recent statutory intervention in the field, it would seem doubtful whether the High Court will intervene again to create further common law exceptions, but the possibility cannot be altogether ruled out, in view of the wide power of the Court to intervene in criminal matters.

English law

As the passage from *Subramaniam* (above) shows, English law also maintains a distinction between primary and secondary hearsay. In England, however, the hearsay rule is somewhat wider in scope than the Scots rule. In particular, the English rule categorises as inadmissible hearsay statements from which information can be *implied*, as well as those which explicitly assert some fact. Thus, for example, the statement in *McLaren v. McLeod*, above, would be inadmissible in England in so far as it implied that the house in which it was overheard was in fact a brothel. (Although compare the case of *Woodhouse v. Hall* (1980). The evidence was, of course, relevant in *McLaren* only in so far as it implied exactly that).

The most recent example of this aspect of the rule in England is the well-known case of *R. v. Kearley* (1992). In that case, the Crown sought to lead evidence of certain telephone calls and visits made to a house during a police search for controlled drugs. The callers had all asked for the appellant, "Chippie", and asked to be supplied with drugs. None of the telephone callers or visitors were called as witnesses, and the Crown sought instead to rely on police evidence of the calls. This was objected to as hearsay, an objection which the House of Lords ultimately sustained, on the basis that the statements were relevant only in as much as they implied that Chippie was a supplier of drugs. Two dissenting opinions were delivered in *Kearley*, however, and it would appear that these opinions are the ones which would be followed in Scotland. In *Lord Advocate's Reference (No. 1 of 1992)* (1992), Lord Justice General Hope said that the grounds for the dissenting opinions delivered in *Kearley*: "would cause no surprise in Scotland [since] the evidence in question was *direct* evidence of a relevant fact, that is to say the existence of potential customers willing and anxious to purchase drugs at the premises from the defendant."

On this view there is no infringement of the hearsay rule because the statement is relevant in itself, and is not being used testimonially. Nothing is really asserted or narrated by the statement "Give me some drugs please". To forbid statements from which information may be implied about the facts in issue would seem a hopelessly wide formulation of the rule, since evidence about a statement from which nothing could be implied or inferred about the facts in issue would be irrelevant. The cases of *Lord Advocate's Reference (No. 1 of 1992)* and *McLaren v. McLeod*, above, make it reasonably clear that this does not, in any event, represent the law of Scotland.

The *res gestae*

A statement which would normally be excluded by the hearsay rule will be admitted if it forms part of the *res gestae*—the "whole thing that happened". The idea here is that a statement may be so closely associated with an event that (a) the statement seems entirely likely to be spontaneous, having been forced from the witness by the pressure of the circumstances (compare *O'Hara v. Central SMT Co.* (1941)), and (b) it would be artificial or even misleading to look at evidence of the event without also considering the terms of the statement (*Teper v. R.* (1952)). Where evidence is admitted as part of the *res gestae* it is admitted as secondary hearsay—testimonially—and becomes part of the evidence in the case. However, the connection—particularly in terms of time—with the events in question must be close. In *Teper v. R.*, for example, the appellant was charged with deliberately setting fire to his own shop to defraud his insurers. A police officer gave evidence that he had heard a woman shouting "your place burning and you going away from the fire" some 26 minutes after the fire was said to have started. This evidence was held to be inadmissible because it was insufficiently contemporaneous with the event in question. In *O'Hara* a statement by a bus driver was admitted some 12 minutes after he had been involved in a road accident, but this appears to have been on the basis that the statement was made at the first opportunity for the release of his pent-up emotion, and could safely be regarded as spontaneous.

Confessions

Where someone makes a statement which is self-incriminating, evidence about that statement is usually admissible, since it is thought that people will not usually make a statement which is against their own interests unless that statement is true. While this premise may be open to doubt, there is no question that secondary evidence of confessions *is* admissible in spite of its undoubted status as hearsay. If a confession is held to be inadmissible, it is usually because it was unfairly or improperly obtained, and this question is addressed in the next section.

Self-serving statements

By contrast with confessions, self-serving statements are usually inadmissible because the risk of fabrication is thought to be too high. However, where a self-serving statement is led by the Crown—and the accused's reply to caution and charge is almost always so led, whether it is self-serving or incriminating—it is admissible as evidence in the case; that is, it is admissible "testimonially" as evidence of the truth of its contents. "Mixed" statements are statements which are capable of being regarded as both incriminating and exculpatory—"I shot the Sheriff, but I swear it was in self-defence" would be an example of such a statement. If such a statement is led, either by the Crown, or by the defence with the consent of the Crown, then the whole statement is admissible as an exception to the hearsay rule (*Morrison v. H.M. Advocate* (1990)). Formerly (thanks to cases such as *Hendry v. H.M. Advocate* (1986)) only the incriminating part was admissible, a situation regarded by the High Court in *Morrison* as "obviously unfair". In any other case, a statement which is to any extent self-serving is admissible *only* to show that the accused has told a consistent story throughout the proceedings (thus bolstering his credibility) and not as evidence in the case. Extra-judicial statements made by one accused cannot, however, be used as evidence in favour of another person accused in the same proceedings (*Mathieson v. H.M. Advocate* (1996)).

The Criminal Justice (Scotland) Act 1995

As a result of recommendations by the Scottish Law Commission, the hearsay rule in criminal proceedings was substantially modified by the Criminal Justice (Scotland) Act 1995. The relevant provisions are now contained in the Criminal Procedure (Scotland) Act 1995, ss. 259–263.

Section 259 sets out the principal rules introduced by the Act. As well as the exceptions mentioned above, hearsay is admissible under the Act if the maker of the statement:

- is dead or is physically or mentally unfit to give evidence. This extends the common rule which allowed hearsay only where the maker of a statement was dead or permanently insane;
- is named and identified, but is outwith the United Kingdom and cannot reasonably be brought to court;

- is named and identified, but cannot be found. Formerly, if a witness disappeared it was simply a misfortune which the litigant just had to put up with (*H.M. Advocate v. Monson* (1893));
- refuses, whether lawfully or otherwise, to swear the oath or to give evidence in court. Section 261 of the Act provides that a co-accused who declines to give evidence may be treated as refusing to give evidence for the purposes of section 259. Taken together, these provisions partially overrule the effect of *McLay v. H.M. Advocate* (1994), which held that a confession by a person other than the accused was not admissible as an exception to the hearsay rule. It *will* now be possible to lead such evidence if the conditions imposed by the 1995 Act are satisfied, which in such cases seems highly likely.

There are certain pre-conditions which must also be satisfied before section 259 can operate:

- that the person who made the statement will not give evidence in the proceedings for any of the reasons given above;
- that evidence of the matter would be admissible if the maker of the statement were to give direct oral evidence of it. Thus, hearsay would not be admissible if a statement in any event was privileged or constituted a precognition;
- that the maker of the statement would have been a competent witness at the time the statement was made. This provision contrasts with the Civil Evidence (Scotland) Act 1988 which, in permitting hearsay evidence, does not specify the time at which the maker of the statement in question must be regarded as competent (see Civil Evidence).
- that there is sufficient evidence that a particular statement was made, and is either contained in a document, or is one of which the person giving evidence about the statement has direct personal knowledge.

Adoption of prior statements—section 260

Section 260 of the Act deals with prior statements made by a person who is a witness in the proceedings. The section provides that where a prior statement is contained in a document, and the witness says in evidence that the statement was made by him and that he adopts it as his evidence, then the prior statement will be admissible "testimonially". This is said to be a statutory form of the rule contained in the case of *Jameson v. H.M. Advocate (No. 2)* (1994). To understand this, it is necessary to look at a number of cases dealing with evidence of prior identification made by a witness. (It should be noted here that the common law rules are specifically preserved by section 262(4).)

Evidence of previous identification and the rule in *Muldoon v. Herron*

In *Muldoon v. Herron* (1970), three youths were charged with a breach of the peace. At their trial the only two eyewitnesses to the offence gave evidence that, soon after the offence was committed, they had pointed out to the police several of those involved. Neither witness identified the accused in court and one said that the accused were not among those she had pointed out as being among those implicated. The sheriff-substitute disbelieved her. Two police officers gave evidence that the accused *were* among those pointed out and those witnesses were believed by the sheriff-substitute. The High Court held, on appeal, that the evidence of the police was just as "direct and primary" on the matter of *who* was identified as that of the original witnesses themselves. The police evidence was therefore permitted to supplement or replace the evidence of the witness, in spite of her insistence that her earlier statement or identification was inaccurate.

In England, this *is* regarded as a situation involving conflict with the hearsay rule (*R v. Osborne and Virtue* (1973)), on the basis that what is being given is a second-hand account of an extra-judicial statement. Moreover, there is certainly a "best evidence" problem, since the original witness clearly cannot be cross-examined as to the reliability of her identification. The opinions in *Muldoon* do deal with the hearsay point, but suggest that the police evidence was admissible as *primary* hearsay. On this view the identification was admissible as original evidence that a statement was made. As we have seen above, the fact that the identification contains an implication that the person pointed out was the perpetrator is immaterial, since the hearsay rule in Scotland is confined to matter explicitly asserted in a statement.

However, it seems that, whatever *Muldoon* may say, there is no hearsay aspect to this rule at all. The doctrine merely allows the filling of a gap in the evidence of a witness who cannot recall exactly whom he identified, or indeed, what he said, since the rule now applies not merely to evidence of identifications, but also to statements or descriptions given by a witness to the police (*Frew v. Jessop* (1990)). In *Jameson v. H.M. Advocate (No. 2)* (1994), it was said that:

> "The *Muldoon* case dealt with the position of a missing link in evidence of identification ... In our opinion the principle upon which the evidence of identification was held to be admissible in that case is of wider application and is not confined to identification evidence. Where a person identifies the alleged culprit to police officers, he is in effect telling them what he saw. He is making a statement to the police officers which is a statement of fact and ought, if possible, to be spoken to by the witness in the witness box. But if he is unable to recollect what he said to the police when he comes to give evidence, the gap in his recollection can be filled by what the police said he said to them at the time. This evidence, when taken with the witness's own evidence that he made a true statement at the time to the police, is held to be admissible because there are two primary sources of evidence. One is the evidence of the police officers as to who was in fact identified and the other is the witness's own evidence that he identified the culprit to the police. The consistency between these two pieces of evidence provides the link between them and completes the chain".

This analysis of *Muldoon* depends on the original witness being present in court and giving evidence that although he cannot recollect what he said to the police, he nevertheless accepts the earlier statement as representing his evidence in court. *Jameson* therefore casts doubt on the application of *Muldoon* in those cases such as *Smith v. H.M. Advocate* (1986), in which the witness identifies *someone* to the police, but later denies that his identification was accurate. This cannot be described as an "adoption" of the witness's previous statement (section 260 of the 1995 Act is said to be a statutory version of the common law rules). Where the witness does have some recollection of the statement, and denies its accuracy, then there is no "link" or "gap" capable of being added to or completed by police evidence. It is accordingly arguable that *Jameson* represents a restriction of the *Muldoon* doctrine.

Further reading:

Scottish Law Commission, *Report on Hearsay Evidence in Criminal Proceedings* (Scot. Law Com., No. 149) (1995).
D.H. Sheldon, "Remembrance of Things Past", 1992 S.L.T. (News) 9.
D.H. Sheldon, "The Hearsay Rule Devoured...", 1995 J.R. 504.
A.B. Wilkinson, "Hearsay: A Scottish Perspective" in *Justice and Crime: Essays in Honour of the Right Honourable The Lord Emslie* (R.F. Hunter ed., T&T Clark, 1993).
A.B. Wilkinson, "The Hearsay Rule in Scotland", 1982 J.R. 213.

III. EVIDENCE UNFAIRLY OR IMPROPERLY OBTAINED

The manner in which evidence is obtained may have an important effect on its admissibility. This section looks first at the admissibility of real and documentary evidence where it is alleged to have been improperly obtained, and then at the admissibility of statements made by the accused. There are theoretical questions here as to the propriety of using the law of evidence as a vehicle for controlling the executive or the police. Should relevant evidence be excluded for this reason? In the English case of *Jones v. Owen* (1870), Mellor J. said that "It would be a dangerous obstacle to the administration of justice if we were to hold, because evidence was obtained by illegal means, it could not be used against a party charged with an offence". In general, English law does *not* therefore regard evidence as inadmissible merely because of some impropriety in the way it was obtained (although see the Police and Criminal Evidence Act 1984, s.78). By contrast, Scots law attempts to reach a compromise between the public interest in the suppression of crime and the public interest in ensuring that the accused is treated fairly. The vehicle which it uses to do this is the test of fairness—was what was done fair to the accused in the circumstances? It is, however, a bilateral test, and in looking at the question of fairness, the interests of the state may also be considered (*Miln v. Cullen* (1967)).

Real and documentary evidence

The recovery of real or documentary evidence will usually involve the necessity of going on to premises occupied by the accused to search for and remove material thought to be incriminating. Indeed searches may sometimes have to be made of the accused's clothing or body. Given the obvious invasion of the accused person's rights that this involves, a warrant must generally be obtained for such searches. There may in some cases be a statutory warrant for such searches—for example, the Misuse of Drugs Act 1971, s.23(2) gives the police power to search anyone whom they reasonably suspect of being in possession of controlled drugs. Questions frequently arise as to whether a search was permissible or justifiable in any given case. Whether the search is carried out by police officers or others, the test for admissibility would appear to be the same. In *Wilson v. Brown* (1996), a man described as a "patron" at a rave was stopped and searched by stewards against his will. He was found to be in possession of temazepam "jellies" and was detained by the stewards until the police could be called. It was held that the search was illegal and could not be excused on any ground, although the court did say that it might have been different had weapons and not drugs been found. From this case, it can be seen that a number of factors play a part in decisions on admissibility. The presence of a formal power to conduct a search is only one of these.

The basic rule is contained in the case of *Lawrie v. Muir* (1950). That case holds that, in general, evidence which is obtained improperly must be excluded. However, irregularities may be overlooked in some circumstances:

> "Whether any given irregularity ought to be excused depends upon the nature of the irregularity and the circumstances under which it was committed. In particular, the case may bring into play the discretionary principle of fairness to the accused which has been developed so fully in our law in relation to the admission in evidence of confessions or admissions by a person suspected or charged with crime. That principle would obviously require consideration in any case in which the departure from the strict procedure had been adopted deliberately with a view to securing the admission of evidence obtained by an unfair trick. Again, there are many statutory offences in relation to which Parliament has prescribed in detail in the interests of fairness a special procedure to be followed in obtaining evidence; and in such cases ... it is very easy to see why a departure from the strict rules has often been held to be fatal to the prosecution's case. On the other hand, to take an extreme instance figured in argument, it would usually be wrong to exclude some highly incriminating production in a murder trial merely because it was found by a police officer in the course of a search authorised for a different purpose or before a proper warrant had been obtained".

In *Lawrie v. Muir*, inspectors from the Milk Marketing Board inadvertently misrepresented their authority to search certain premises. This misrepresentation was said to be enough to justify the exclusion of the evidence. However, there are various circumstances in which evidence which has been recovered in apparent violation of the proper procedures *will* be admissible.

Warrants

Warrants will normally be granted during the course of a criminal investigation to search the accused's home or business premises, and provided that the police search within the terms of the warrant, any evidence found as a result will be admissible. However, the terms of a warrant will usually be strictly enforced by the courts. While minor defects in a warrant will often be excused, errors in the essentials of a warrant will usually be fatal. In *H.M. Advocate v. Cumming* (1983), for example, a warrant was granted under section 23(2) of the Misuse of Drugs Act 1971. A discrepancy between the name of the person specified in the deposition of the warrant and the name of the accused was not fatal to the warrant's validity; nor was a failure to date the warrant, since a date had been appended by a Justice of the Peace who had signed the warrant. A failure in the warrant to specify the police officer who had authority under the warrant to conduct the search was described as being a breach of section 23(2), however, as was a failure to specify the premises to be searched. These defects taken together were fatal to the validity of the warrant, and items recovered under the warrant were held to be inadmissible.

Statutory warrants will also be interpreted strictly, and, as *Lawrie v. Muir* suggests, any failure to adhere to a statutory procedure may well result in the exclusion of evidence. *Ireland v. Russell* (1995) provides an example. The Misuse of Drugs Act 1971, s.23(2) gives the police power to search individuals on reasonable suspicion of their possession of controlled drugs. In *Ireland v. Russell*, the police had received information that the accused was in possession of cannabis. It was not until some two months after this information was received that they were able to stop and search him. The accused in fact proved to be in possession of drugs, and the question arose as to whether the police were entitled in the circumstances to conduct the search on the basis of "reasonable suspicion". It was held that they were not, given the lapse of time between the receipt of the information and the search.

There are exceptions to this strict approach—in *McCarron v. Allen* (1988), for example, a person who came to the door of a property which was being searched under warrant, was said to have been "found" on those premises for the purposes of section 23(2) of the Misuse of Drugs Act 1971. Moreover, if a search can be justified by a statutory provision, it may not matter that the search was actually being carried out under different authority. In *Burke v. Wilson* (1988), police carrying out a search for unclassified videos under the terms of the Video Recordings Act 1984 discovered and removed certain obscene videos which contravened section 51 of the Civic Government (Scotland) Act 1982. The videos were admitted in evidence even although the warrant for the search had been granted under the 1984 and not the 1982 Act. It is also clear that if there is statutory power to search, there is no need to ask a suspect for his permission to conduct a search, or to warn him that he might have a right to refuse (*Chassar v. Macdonald* (1996)). In the final analysis, however, it would appear that the matter may be boiled down to a question of "fairness", and the balance referred to in *Lawrie v. Muir* between the competing interests in the criminal justice system. There are few absolute rules here.

Personal searches and bodily samples
The arrest of a suspect provides sufficient warrant for non-invasive searches of the accused's person and clothing, and the taking of fingerprints and swabs for the purpose of DNA testing (*Adair v. McGarry* (1933); Criminal Procedure (Scotland) Act 1995, s.18). However, it seems that fingerprints taken in relation to one offence will be admitted even if the accused has been arrested only in relation to another (*Namyslak v. H.M. Advocate* (1994)). More invasive or radical searches require specific authorisation. Warrants may be granted, for example, for the taking of dental impressions (*Hay v. H.M. Advocate* (1968)) or blood samples (*Milford v. H.M. Advocate* (1973)). Again, the factors to be weighed by the court in deciding whether or not to grant such a warrant include the seriousness of the offence, and the degree to which the proposed procedure infringes the liberty or bodily integrity of the suspect.

Stumbling and fishing
When carrying out a search, officers must stay within the boundaries of the authority set out in the warrant. In *McAvoy v. Jessop* (1988), for example, the police obtained a warrant to search for a stolen video recorder in a house occupied by the appellant's brother at a named address. That house proved to be a flat which was divided into a number of separately occupied bedsitting-rooms, one of which was occupied by the appellant and one of which was occupied by her brother. When the police discovered that the appellant's brother was not in his room, they showed the warrant to the appellant who did not object to a search of her room. The stolen video recorder was discovered in the appellant's room and she was charged with resetting it. The magistrate repelled an objection to the admissibility of evidence of the finding of the video recorder on the view that what occurred was analogous to the search of different rooms in a family home. On appeal to the High Court it was held that the warrant could not reasonably be read as extending to any premises except those actually occupied by the appellant's brother and the search of the appellant's room was therefore illegal.

This principle also applies to the offence to which the warrant relates. Where a warrant authorises the police to search for the proceeds of a particular house-breaking, for example, their authority to search does not extend to items stolen on another occasion. Any deliberate attempt to go "fishing" for evidence without specific warrant to search will render evidence inadmissible (*H.M. Advocate v. Turnbull* (1951)). On the other hand, where the police are lawfully engaged in a search, and in the course of that search they inadvertently stumble upon material which is plainly incriminating or at least suspicious, then the new material may well be admissible (*H.M. Advocate v. Hepper* (1958)). In determining the question of admissibility in such circumstances therefore, much may depend upon what police witnesses say at trial about their intentions when carrying out a search. In *Drummond v. H.M. Advocate* (1992), two police officers conducted a search of the accused's house under a warrant allowing them to search for goods stolen from a furniture store in Edinburgh. In the course of the search they found, hidden in a wardrobe, items of clothing stolen from premises in Penicuik and the accused was subsequently charged with the theft of that clothing. One of the officers said that he had opened the wardrobe suspecting that it might contain the stolen clothing. His evidence was ruled to be inadmissible since the warrant did not cover those items and he had deliberately set out to look for them. The other officer said that he had been looking for smaller items stolen from the Edinburgh theft, and had stumbled upon the clothing by accident. His evidence was admitted.

Again, in *Baxter v. Scott* (1992), the accused was arrested in connection with a motoring offence and the police took possession of his car. They opened the boot of the car and found a number of stolen items in it. This evidence was admitted on the basis that no search had taken place at all. The police were said to be entitled to check the contents of the car, since they were responsible for both car and contents while it remained in their custody. In *Graham v. Orr* (1995), on the other hand, the police became suspicious of the accused when he was detained on another motoring charge and an officer conducted a search of his car. Evidence of the controlled drugs which they found in the car was ruled inadmissible because there had been no authority for the search. This case implies that cars may count as premises and that accordingly there is no automatic right to search them when an accused person is arrested or detained, even in relation to a motoring offence. Any search must be justified either by a warrant or statutory power, or by reference to the sort of "security check" which took place in *Baxter v. Scott*.

Finally, it seems that the police must be aware of any limits imposed by the warrant. If they are not, then inevitably any search which they carry out is one conducted without limits, and is *ex hypothesi* unauthorised (see *Leckie v. Miln* (1982)). Thus, if a warrant permits the police to search for the proceeds of a particular house-breaking but the officers who execute the warrant are unaware of the conditions it sets, any search which they purport to carry out under the warrant is apparently an unlimited one, and therefore illegal, unless in the unlikely event of the householder giving specific consent to an unlimited search.

Urgency

Where there is a risk that evidence will be lost unless a search is carried out immediately, search without a warrant will usually be justified. In *H.M. Advocate v. McGuigan* (1936), for example, police carried out a search of a tent occupied by the accused's parents shortly after the accused was arrested and charged with rape and murder. Evidence recovered during the search was held to be admissible in spite of the fact that the search had been carried out without a warrant. In this case the offence was a very serious one and there was clearly an imminent likelihood that evidence might be destroyed or tampered with. In *Walsh v. Macphail* (1978), on the other hand, a search was made for cannabis on a military air-base without a valid warrant. Evidence of the proceeds of that search was admitted even although the suspects were subject to military discipline and were denied access to the accommodation blocks where the drugs were thought to be. Given the relatively trivial nature of the offence concerned, and the ease with which a proper warrant could have been obtained without an accompanying risk that the suspects might tamper with the evidence, it is arguable that in this case the balance of fairness should have led to the exclusion of the evidence. Similarly, in the case of *Webley v. Ritchie* (1997) evidence recovered when the police forced open the accused's car was admitted, in spite of the absence of a warrant. The police claimed that they did not know how long it would have taken to obtain a warrant, since they were unfamiliar with local procedures. In addition, they did not want to leave a junior colleague to guard the vehicle while a warrrant was obtained, since she was "inexperienced". As with *Walsh*, the feeling remains that the concept of urgency has been stretched a very long way from its application in older cases such as *McGuigan*.

Undercover operations
Where police officers pose as ordinary citizens in order to obtain evidence of wrongdoing, there is clearly an element of deception or misrepresentation. However, it would appear that provided that the deception does not go beyond certain limits, evidence obtained as a result of such undercover operations will be admissible. In a number of cases involving the supply of controlled drugs, evidence of the transactions has been admitted where the police officers concerned have held themselves out to be members of the public, and in some cases given false information to convince the suspect of their "bona fides" (*H.M. Advocate v. Harper* (1987), *Weir v. Jessop (No. 2)* (1991)). Should the authorities offer inducements or threats in order to persuade a suspect to enter into a particular transaction, however, it is likely that this would go beyond the boundaries of fairness and render any resultant evidence inadmissible.

Consent
The consent of the person searched may render legal a search for which there is otherwise no proper warrant. *McGovern v. H.M. Advocate* (1950) takes a fairly liberal view of the issue of consent, appearing to lay down a rule which approaches a requirement for informed consent in the criminal law. The High Court said that, where the police had taken scrapings from the accused's fingernails prior to arrest and charge, "no consent would avail ... unless it was given after a fair intimation that the consent could be withheld". The more recent cases of *Davidson v. Brown* (1990) and *Devlin v. Normand* (1992), however, cast some doubt on this approach.

In *Devlin*, for example, the accused had hidden a packet of cannabis resin in her mouth. Without cautioning her, or informing her under what authority he was doing so (such as the Misuse of Drugs Act 1971 or the Prisons (Scotland) Act 1989), a prison officer required her to open her mouth and lift her tongue, which she did without objection. Evidence of this incident and of the finding of the drug was objected to on the ground that it constituted an illegal search. This argument was rejected on appeal, the High Court taking the view that the procedure followed did not amount to a search, but simply to a suspect voluntarily complying with a request. There was no reference in this case to *McGovern* or to any requirement that the prison officer should have informed the suspect of any right to decline to open her mouth. In *Davidson v. Brown*, *McGovern* was distinguished on the basis that while in the earlier case the accused was clearly a suspect and was about to be questioned under caution as to his involvement in the incident concerned, in the later case the accused was not a suspect and in any event there was no search, only a non-mandatory request for information. This, of course, rather begs the question of how the accused could have known that the request was non-mandatory, but at all events it seems that as with the questioning of a suspect (as to which see below), the law gives more protection to one who has clearly fallen under suspicion, than to a person who is not yet at the centre of any particular investigation.

Difficulties over the question of consent appear to have been resolved by the recent case of *Brown v. Glen* (1997). In that case, it was held that a person who is asked by the police to submit to a search or to hand over some article for examination, need not usually be informed of their right to refuse. Only where the person is in the position of a suspect, such as the accused in *McGovern* does any such warning need to be given. The law in this area is thus brought largely into line with that in relation to the cautioning of suspects prior to or during questioning.

As with search under warrant, however, officers carrying out a search on the basis of consent must do so within the limits of the consent given. The limits of that consent are to be judged by reference to the information possessed by the searched person and not that of the searchers. If the police do not know the precise terms of a warrant, as in *Leckie v. Miln* (1982), then in order to render their search lawful, they would have to request and receive consent for a search unlimited by any reference to particular offences or items.

Police questioning and the admissibility of incriminating statements

As with the recovery of real and documentary evidence, the principle governing the admissibility of extra-judicial admissions and confessions is the principle of fairness. Again, this is a bilateral test, taking into account both fairness to the accused, and the interests of the state in securing the conviction of offenders. It is, however, a vague and flexible test, and the attitude of the High Court has oscillated over the years between liberal and "law and order" interpretations of the rule. Accordingly, analysis in this area has to be strongly case based, there being few fixed rules upon which to rely.

Chalmers v. H.M. Advocate (1954) is the "hardy perennial" case on the admissibility of confessions. In that case, the High Court distinguished between three stages of a criminal investigation at which the law gives differing degrees of protection to the accused. In the initial stages of an investigation, before suspicion has centred on any particular person, the police may question anyone with a view to acquiring information about the offence; but secondly, once suspicion has "crystallised" then officers must be very careful in questioning the suspect further. At that stage "[f]urther interrogation of that person becomes very dangerous, and, if carried too far, e.g. to the point of extracting a confession by what amounts to cross-examination, the evidence of that confession will almost certainly be excluded".

Giving the leading opinion, Lord Cooper does mention that the principle of fairness was the "ultimate test of the propriety or otherwise of admitting self-incriminating evidence" in such circumstances. A more important element in his opinion, however, was the idea that since an accused person is not a compellable witness against himself, to allow the extraction of a confession, and its later admission at trial, would in effect be to force the accused to give evidence against himself, at second hand as it were. Accordingly, a crucial consideration in determining the admissibility of a confession was whether or not the statement was made voluntarily. Thirdly, once a person has been charged, then all questioning must cease in relation to the subject-matter of the charge, and the accused must be brought before a court at the earliest opportunity. It is, however, only the formal process of charging an accused with a crime that activates this third, most stringent level of protection. In *H.M. Advocate v. Pender* (1996) there was a break in the questioning of a robbery suspect while the police "formulated a charge". The accused made a lengthy and incriminating statement on the resumption of the interview, and this was held to be admissible, in spite of the break and the reason for it.

Broadly speaking, the rules as to stages one and three have survived intact. At stage one, the question of fairness may still be a live issue, however, and it is possible that something may be said or done at that stage resulting in unfairness to an accused person, and the exclusion of any statement made (see *Miln v. Cullen* (1967)). Moreover, it has recently been held that arrest and charge do not necessarily go together, so that a person may be arrested, but not charged, thus "freezing" the procedure at stage two for the purposes of questioning (*Johnston v. H.M. Advocate* (1993)). It is the second stage—the stage at which a suspect is "helping the police with their inquiries", in modern practice usually under the statutory detention procedures now contained in the Criminal Procedure (Scotland) Act 1995—that most controversy has arisen. While the emphasis in *Chalmers* was on the need for a statement which was made voluntarily and spontaneously, cases such as *Hartley v. H.M. Advocate*, (1979) and *Lord Advocate's Reference (No. 1 of 1983)* (1984) focused on the "simple and intelligible test which has worked well in practice—has what has taken place been fair or not?" These cases turned on the broad, bilateral view of "fairness" apparently espoused in cases such as *Miln v. Cullen*, above. In this revision of *Chalmers*, fairly vigourous questioning *is* allowed. In *Lord Advocate's Reference (No. 1 of 1983)* Lord Justice General Emslie said that:

> "For the avoidance of doubt I should add that where in the opinions in the decided cases the word 'interrogation' or the expression 'cross-examination' are used in discussing unfair tactics on the part of the police, they are to be understood to refer only to improper forms of questioning tainted with an element of bullying or pressure designed to break the will of the suspect or to force from him a confession against his will".

However, it may be that the High Court is moving back towards an interpretation of "fairness" which has more in common with *Chalmers* than with the later cases. In *Codona v. H.M. Advocate* (1996), a 14-year-old girl was convicted of murder, largely on the strength of confession evidence obtained after a lengthy interrogation in which she was reduced to tears and questioned in such a way as "to demonstrate an intention [on the part of the police] to extract from her admissions about her participation in the assault which she clearly was not willing to make voluntarily". Lord Justice General Hope continued:

> "[The 'fairness' test] must never be permitted to become a formality, especially where the suspect, due to age or mental impairment or other disability, may be vulnerable under police questioning. It is important to remember that the accused is not a compellable witness at his or her own trial. Fairness demands that he or she should not be induced or forced by police questioning to make a statement to them which is incriminating. As Lord Hunter said in *H.M. Advocate v. Mair* ... in order that a statement made by an accused person to the police may be available as evidence against him, it must be truly spontaneous and voluntary. The police may question a suspect, but when they move into the field of cross-examination or interrogation, they move into an area of great difficulty. If the questioning is carried too far, by means of leading or repetitive questioning or by pressure in other ways in an effort to obtain from the suspect what they are seeking to obtain from him, the statement is likely to be excluded on the ground that it was extracted by unfair means. Lord Justice-General Emslie's definition of the words 'interrogation' and 'cross-examination' in *Lord Advocate's Reference (No. 1 of 1983)* at p.69, as referring only to improper forms of questioning tainted with an element of bullying or pressure designed to break the will of the suspect or to force from him a confession against his will, should not be understood as implying any weakening of these important principles."

Inevitably, the view which is taken about "fairness" will vary from case to case. However, certain specific issues may be identified.

The need for a caution

In the older cases, it seems to have been accepted that before a statement could be regarded as fairly obtained, a caution had to be administered. That is, the accused had to be warned that he or she need not say anything in reply to police questioning, but that anything which they did say could be used in evidence at their trial. This view was in keeping with the *Chalmers* emphasis on the need for a voluntary statement. More recent cases emphasise that the need for a caution is simply a matter for assessment in each case, on the basis of the fairness test (*Pennycuick v. Lees* (1992)). It may be that only in fairly extreme cases, such as those in which there is a clear breach of the rules of fairness in questioning, will the absence of a caution be fatal.

In *Tonge v. H.M. Advocate* (1982), for example, police officers effectively charged the accused with complicity in the offence being investigated, saying that they had "reason to believe that he was responsible, along with others, for the crime". At that time, the accused

against him. They learned that a witness, R, was to have a business meeting with the accused and arranged for a radio transmitter to be concealed in R's clothing to record their conversation. Evidence of this recording was excluded, Lord Cameron holding that the rules of fairness and fair dealing had been flagrantly transgressed. Had the questions put to the accused been asked by the police, a caution would almost certainly have been necessary, and the fact that it was a civilian performing the interrogation could not render admissible what would otherwise have been excluded. *H.M. Advocate v. Campbell* (1964) was a similar case, except that, rather than using a concealed transmitter, a plain clothes police officer eavesdropped on a conversation between the accused and a newspaper reporter. Again, no caution was administered to the accused, and his admission of involvement in the murder under investigation was ruled inadmissible.

There are suggestions in *Weir v. Jessop (No. 2)* (1991) that *Campbell* (and impliedly therefore, *Graham*) was wrongly decided, and that since the statement was made voluntarily and without inducements from or cross-examination by the police it would, in modern practice, be regarded as admissible. Such suggestions are, however, *obiter*, and in any event, *Weir v. Jessop (No. 2)* concerned a very different situation from that in *Campbell*, in which the police were attempting (admittedly by means of a subterfuge) to obtain evidence of the actual commission of a crime. In the earlier case of *Hopes and Lavery v. H.M. Advocate* (1960), which was distinguished in *Graham*, evidence of a tape-recording was admitted in relation to a charge of blackmail. The tape recorded a conversation between the accused and the intended victim, in which the accused had actually attempted to extort money from the latter. Lord Justice General Clyde said:

> "It was suggested that there was something improper or underhand in eavesdropping of this kind. But, if this kind of crime is to be stopped methods such as the present one are necessary to detect and prove a particularly despicable type of crime, which is practised in secret and away from observation. It hardly lies in the mouth of a blackmailer to complain that the jury are told the truth about his conversation when he is exerting pressure on his cornered victim. His remedy is not to blackmail. In my opinion, therefore, the Inspector's evidence regarding the conversation was perfectly competent."

There is, in other words, no need to caution someone not to commit a crime. In the cases of *Campbell* and *Graham*, by contrast, the crime had already been committed. Accordingly, the suspects should have been cautioned or put on notice as to the purpose of the conversations into which they were being inveigled.

Where, on the other hand, an admission or confession is *accidentally* overheard by police, rather than deliberately "gathered", then, other things being equal, the statement will be admissible. In *Jamieson v. Annan* (1988), a police officer overheard two accused persons shouting to each other in the cells. The incriminating statements which they made were admitted on the basis that there was no trap, no inducement and no unfairness to the accused in the circumstances. The case does suggest, however, that had the police deliberately "bugged" the cells in order to obtain incriminating material, then any resultant statements might well have been excluded.

Threats and inducements

It is probably impossible to list all of the ways in which a statement might be rendered inadmissible. Actual violence offered by the police to a suspect would be an obvious, if extreme, example. A more subtle variation, however, is where the accused is offered some form of inducement, or some threat is made which might lead him to make a confession. (It should be noted that there is no need for an actual causal connection between the inducement and the confession—*Black v. Annan* (1995); it is enough that the inducement was calculated to lead to a confession.) In *Black v. Annan*, above, for example, a person was detained on a Saturday in connection with a charge of reset. He was told that if he did not provide the police with information about the offence he would be arrested and held in the cells until he could be brought before a court on the following Monday. In these circumstances the statement made by the accused was held to be inadmissible. Again, in *Harley v. H.M. Advocate* (1995), the police told the accused, in effect, that if he did not co-operate, the police would reveal his adultery to the husband of a woman with whom he had been associating. Once again, his incriminating statement was held to be inadmissible because of the police's infringement of the "rules of fairness and fair dealing".

Conclusions

It would appear that the over-arching test of fairness is one which is not only highly flexible and susceptible of many differing interpretations, but one which, in addition, contains elements of other tests. Consider, for example, the cases of *Graham* and *Jamieson v. Annan*, above, in one of which evidence of an incriminating statement was admitted; in the other, excluded. Arguably, however, considerations of fairness to the accused are equal in these cases since in neither case was the accused cautioned; in neither case were they informed of their right to remain silent; in both cases, the statement was made quite voluntarily and without the exertion of any pressure or the offering of any inducement. Accordingly, the issue in these cases seems to be related more to the acceptability of police methods than to that of fairness to the accused overall. Again, cases such as *Black v. Annan*, above, suggest that the reliability of a confession may be a consideration. This in turn is closely related to the issue of the voluntariness of a confession, which remains an important factor in making the decision as to fairness (*Codona v. H.M. Advocate* (1996)). All or each one of these factors may have to be considered in relation to each individual case. The difficulty of predicting the outcome of cases where "fairness" is in issue is exacerbated by the fact that, in general, fairness is a jury question. It is only in the most extreme cases, where it is clear that no reasonable jury could hold that a statement had been obtained fairly, that the matter will be withdrawn from them (see, *e.g. Balloch v. H.M. Advocate* (1977)).

Civil cases

Scots law as to the admissibility of improperly obtained evidence in civil causes is far from settled. In *Rattray v. Rattray* (1897), two out of four Inner House judges held that improprieties have no effect on admissibility. Lord Trayner said that "the policy of the law in later years (and I think a good policy) has been to admit almost all evidence which will throw light on disputed facts and enable justice to be done". Lord Moncrieff agreed with him. *Rattray* must be regarded as a somewhat dubious authority, however (see the criticisms made by Macphail in *Evidence*, paras. 21–08 to 21–12), not least because it was decided before the law became settled in relation to criminal proceedings. Although, in theory, *Rattray* remains the leading case in this area, it is submitted that the views of Lord Wheatley in the *Duke of Argyll*'s case (*Duke of Argyll v. Duchess of Argyll* (1963)) are preferable. In that case, the Duke broke into the Duchess's house and took diaries which contained material suggestive of adultery. The Lord Ordinary, Lord Wheatley, held the diaries to be admissible, but said further that, contrary to what *Rattray* suggests, there was no fixed rule on the question of admissibility. Instead, admissibility will depend on the particular circumstances of the case, taking into account factors such as "the nature of the evidence concerned, the purpose for which it is used in evidence, the manner in which it was obtained, whether its introduction is fair to the party from whom it has been illegally obtained and whether its admission will in fairness throw light on disputed facts and enable justice to be done". In other words, the case amounts to an adoption into civil procedure of the guidelines set out in criminal cases, and in particular in *Lawrie v. Muir* (1950), which is referred to with approval in Lord Wheatley's opinion. The case of *Oghonoghor v. Secretary of State for the Home Department* (1996) provides more recent evidence of the adoption of these principles into civil procedure, albeit that the case is of a quasi-criminal nature.

Further reading:
W. Finnie, "Police Powers of Search in the Light of *Leckie v. Miln*", 1982 S.L.T. (News) 289.

IV. CHARACTER AND COLLATERAL EVIDENCE

In general, evidence which is "collateral" to the facts in issue is inadmissible. The classification of collateral evidence includes evidence of previous incidents similar or related to the particular event under examination— indeed the English equivalent of collateral evidence is known as "similar fact" evidence. It also includes evidence about the character of the accused person, or of parties to a civil case or other witnesses, and this in turn contains the sub-category of evidence of other criminal acts or acts of wrongdoing by a party. Although this rule is often considered to be an exclusionary rule in the same class as hearsay and evidence improperly obtained, it is arguable that the rule about collateral evidence is simply an aspect of a much more general exclusionary rule; that is, the rule requiring evidence to be (sufficiently) relevant. Thus, if there is a sufficient connection between previous events and the one under consideration—if the previous incidents are sufficiently relevant, in other words—then evidence about those events may well be admissible. In *W. Alexander & Sons v. Dundee Corporation* (1950), discussed above, the pursuer's bus was involved in a crash when it skidded on a certain stretch of road. Evidence was admitted of previous similar accidents which had occurred at the same location as that suffered by the pursuer's bus. The pattern of incidents in this case clearly rendered more likely the pursuer's contention that the road at that particular location had been kept in an unsafe condition. Lord Justice Clerk Thomson said that:

> "It was argued to us that the evidence ought to be excluded because this question of the behaviour of the vehicles is a 'collateral issue' in the sense in which that phrase is used in a number of cases which were cited to us. But if it is established that the skidding of these vehicles on these other occasions was truly due to the condition of the road, then it seems to me that that is not a collateral issue at all but something having a direct bearing on the decision of the present case.

While the relevance of "collateral" evidence plays a crucial part in determining its admissibility, it is important to appreciate that the concept of relevance is not an absolute. There may be degrees of relevance, and indeed the concept may itself be "contaminated" by other factors, such as fairness, prejudice, probative value and even simple expediency. In *A v. B* (1895), the pursuer in a civil case sued the defender for damages, claiming that he had raped her. She averred and sought to lead evidence of other rapes carried out by the defender. Evidence of these previous assaults was excluded as collateral. Lord President Robertson justified the decision in the following way:

> "In pronouncing any averment to be irrelevant to the issue, it is not implied that the matter averred has no bearing at all on the question in hand. For example, if the defender admitted at the trial that he had attempted to ravish those two other women, I think the jury might legitimately hold that this made it the more likely that he ravished the pursuer. But, then, Courts of law are not bound to admit the ascertainment of every disputed fact which may contribute, however slightly or indirectly, towards the solution of the issue to be tried. Regard must be had to the limitations which time and human liability to confusion impose upon the conduct of all trials. Experience shows that it is better to sacrifice the aid which might be got from the more or less uncertain solution of collateral issues, than to spend a great amount of time, and confuse the jury with what, in the end, even supposing it to be certain, has only an indirect bearing on the matter in hand".

It can be seen that the collateral evidence rule is based on a number of different factors, and that the classification of evidence as being collateral or otherwise is to a large extent subjective, or at any rate based on the type of "common-sense" considerations referred to in the chapter on relevance.

What the courts really look for in reaching a decision whether to admit evidence which is said to be collateral is evidence of a close connection or nexus between the previous incidents averred and the present one (*H.M. Advocate v. Joseph* (1929), discussed below). In *Gallagher v. Paton* (1909), an advertising agent was charged with fraud. It was alleged that he had pretended to "a female shop assistant" that her employer paid yearly for an advertisement in a directory, and thus induced her to pay him the sum of 1s. 6d. The prosecutor sought to lead evidence of similar attempts made on the same day as the one libelled in the complaint. This evidence was admitted by the magistrate and the accused was convicted. On appeal to the High Court it was held that the evidence had been competently admitted. Lord McLaren said:

> "When the question is whether the accused person made false statements, knowing the statements to be false, and for the purpose of obtaining money to which he was not entitled, I do not know of any better way of establishing the criminal intention than by proof that he had made similar false statements on the same day to other people, and apparently with the same object ... A false statement made to one person may be explained away, but when a system of false statements is proved, the probability is very great that the statements were designedly made."

The English term for this underlying connection is "striking similarity", and this concept appears to perform the same function as the Scottish tests. Moreover, there are obvious parallels here with the "*Moorov* doctrine", described in Chapter 6 in which evidence of other, similar events is used to confirm or render more probable the particular event in question. In *Moorov*, the various incidents are used to confirm one another, but again it is the underlying similarity, unity or nexus which provides the impetus for that process (compare the English case of *R. v. Kilbourne* (1973)).

Civil cases

The principles enunciated above apply also to civil cases in Scotland. *A v. B*, discussed above, provides one example. *H v. P* (1905), in which the defender in an action for slander was not allowed to lead evidence that, in addition to committing adultery with himself, the pursuer had had adulterous relations with two other men, provides another. Although these cases are complicated by considerations relating to character evidence, they are consistent with the idea that, as in criminal cases, evidence is not admissible where it simply tends to show that someone has committed similar acts on a previous occasion—that the person concerned "goes in for that sort of thing". Where there is evidence of a "course of conduct", of a series of acts which are strikingly similar (see *Whyte v. Whyte* (1884); *Roy v. Pairman* (1958)), or where, as in *W. Alexander v. Dundee Corporation*, discussed above, there is a clear connection between the previous incidents and the present one (see also *Knutzen v. Mauritzen* (1918)), then evidence of those events may be led.

Evidence of other criminal acts

Evidence about previous events or conduct may arise in a slightly different context—that is, where the Crown seek to lead evidence of "collateral" offences committed by an accused person, in order to prove another offence. The acts under consideration here may not be similar to the crime charged or to the incident in question, but nevertheless be connected with it. Where, for example, a person is charged with armed robbery, evidence that the accused person was seen sawing off the barrels of a shotgun is circumstantial evidence which is clearly relevant to the robbery charge. But it is also direct evidence of the commission of another crime, since shortening the barrels of a shotgun is itself an offence.

In line with the general rule on collateral evidence, evidence about other criminal acts performed by an accused person is usually inadmissible. Once again, however, the courts will depart from this rule if it is established that the previous acts are clearly connected with or relevant to the present charge. The accused in *Dumoulin v. H.M. Advocate* (1974), for example, was charged with the murder of his wife by pushing her over a precipice at Salisbury Crags in Edinburgh. Evidence was also admitted, however, that he had first fraudulently obtained money in Germany, and had attempted to do so in Scotland; that he had then used this money to pay the initial premium on a large life insurance policy taken out at his behest by a woman-friend; that he had then married this woman on the same day that he was alleged to have killed her. The nexus between the murder charge and these previous transactions was "clearly sufficiently close", given the obvious motive which the transactions provided, to justify its admission. In the light of this connection, the fact that some of the transactions took place in another country was said to be irrelevant. The same view was taken in *H.M. Advocate v. Joseph* (1929). In that case, the accused was charged with a fraudulent scheme involving the forgery of bank documents and the uttering of them, in Scotland, as genuine. The indictment libelled that in pursuance of this scheme, he had uttered a forged document in an hotel in Brussels. It was objected that it was incompetent to charge a crime committed in Belgium, and that evidence of the Belgian uttering was inadmissible. The trial judge repelled the objection. He said that:

> "It is not disputed that our law does not allow proof of a crime other than that which is libelled merely to establish that it is probable or likely that the accused may have committed the crime charged. But I regard it as settled that evidence in regard to another incident of a similar character may be admitted in proof of a crime charge, notwithstanding that this evidence may incidentally show or tend to show the commission of another crime, provided there be some connection or "nexus", which, in the opinion of the Court, is sufficiently intimate, between the two "incidents". There is ample authority for the view that, if the connection between the incident sought to be proved and the crime libelled is very close in point of

time and character, so that they can hardly be dissociated, the evidence will be admitted".

Evidence of other criminal acts may be led even where averments about them do not appear in the complaint or indictment. Such evidence must, of course, be relevant to the crime charged. However, if:

- the evidence tends to show that the accused is of bad character; or
- the evidence is so different in terms of time, place and character from the offence charged that the accused does not have fair notice that evidence of the additional offence is likely to be led; or
- if the evidence is led with the intention of proving that the accused was in fact guilty of that other crime (as opposed to merely committing a trivial offence as a means of committing the "main" crime),

then the requirement of fair notice dictates that the other crime or crimes should be separately libelled. The leading case is *Nelson v. H.M. Advocate* (1994), from which the principles set out above are derived. In that case the accused was charged with being concerned in the supply of controlled drugs. Evidence was led that when the police attempted to arrest the appellant, he went into a toilet and swallowed a small cellophane-wrapped object. Objection was taken to this on the basis that it was evidence which disclosed an unlibelled offence by the appellant, namely obstructing the police contrary to the Misuse of Drugs Act 1971 by attempting to conceal possession of controlled drugs. This objection was repelled both at first instance and at appellate level. The concealment of the drugs in this case was thought to be purely incidental, although relevant, to the main charge.

Character evidence

Evidence about a person's character is in most cases collateral and inadmissible—the case of *H v. P*, above, is one authority for that proposition. However, special considerations apply to the accused and the complainer in a criminal case, and to the parties to a civil action, and these categories are considered below. Moreover, the prohibition applies only to proof of substantive issues; the character of a witness in so far as it reflects on that witness's credibility, is considered fair game. However, such issues will arise only in cross-examination. It is not usually open to a party to lead evidence about a witness's character.

The complainer

The rule about character evidence in relation to the complainer is a complicated one. Generally, such evidence is collateral and inadmissible. But in cases of murder and assault, the defence may lead evidence that the complainer is or was of a violent or quarrelsome disposition (although in so doing, the accused may open himself to attacks on his own character—see the separate section below). Oddly, however, the defence may not lead evidence of specific acts of violence committed by the complainer or deceased upon the accused or others (*Brady v. H.M. Advocate* (1986)). This rule itself suffers exception where the indictment specifically places the character of the accused in issue. In such circumstances the accused may lead evidence to show that in fact it was the complainer or deceased who exhibited bad character. In *H.M. Advocate v. Kay* (1970), the accused was charged with the murder of her husband. Her defence was one of self-defence—specifically that she reasonably believed "that there was an imminent danger to her life due to an assault intended by the deceased." The indictment included an averment that the accused had previously "evinced malice and ill-will" against the deceased, and had brandished a knife at him and threatened to kill him. In these special circumstances, in which previous acts of violence or threats of violence were alleged against the accused, the accused was permitted to lead evidence that on a number of occasions the complainer had assaulted her to such an extent that she had required hospitalisation.

Sexual character

Evidence about the sexual character of the complainer in a case involving sexual offences was at common law admissible to a limited extent. In *Dickie v. H.M. Advocate* (1897), it was held that while it was open to the accused to prove that the complainer was of "bad moral character", or to prove that "the witness voluntarily yielded to his embraces a short time before the alleged criminal attack", it was not permitted to prove individual acts of "unchastity". This view was in line with the law on character evidence in both civil and criminal cases (compare the cases of *H v. P*, and *Brady v. H.M. Advocate*, dealt with above). The underlying rationale was that evidence was admissible to attack the *credibility* of the witness, but not to suggest that "a female who yields her person to one man will presumably do so to any man—a proposition which is quite untenable". In spite of the existence of such rules, questioning about the complainer's sexual history appears to have become common, in relation to the issues of both credibility *and* consent. The frequency of such attacks led to concern that victims of sexual assault were deterred from making complaints because of their fear of such sustained attempts to discredit them sexually, and following a report by the Scottish Law Commission (SLC No. 78) changes to the law were made in 1985 to restrict the extent to which such questioning would be permitted. Those changes are now embodied in sections 274 and 275 of the 1995 Act. The new provisions apply to more or less any case involving a sexual element, and prohibit questioning designed to elicit evidence which shows or tends to show that the complainer is not of good character in relation to sexual matters, is a prostitute or associates with prostitutes, or has engaged in any sexual behaviour which does not form part of the charge. The Act provides a number of exceptions, however. Thus, questioning about sexual history or character is permitted where:

- the questioning is designed to rebut evidence led by someone other than the accused. This means that if the Crown attempt to show that the complainer is of particularly good sexual character, or was a virgin, something which is sometimes regarded as an aggravation to a charge of rape, then the accused may lead evidence in rebuttal;

- the questioning concerns sexual behaviour which took place on the same occasion as the sexual behaviour which is the subject of the charge. This reflects the idea expressed in *Dickie* that it would be relevant to show that the complainer had sexually "yielded" to the accused shortly before the alleged incident, or that it formed part of wider sexual context, such as participation in sexual behaviour as part of a group. It also accords with the common law notion of the *res gestae*—the idea that evidence is admissible about everything which happened on the same occasion, or as part of the same event;
- the questioning is relevant to a defence of incrimination. Here the accused is arguing that someone else was responsible for the sexual assault, and in order to make out that defence, clearly he may have to question the complainer as to whether she indulged in (or suffered) sexual behaviour with someone else;
- it would be contrary to the interests of justice to exclude the questioning. This exception is problematic, as it grants the court a wide discretion to admit evidence of sexual character where it sees fit to do so. A recent (and apparently controversial) study indicates that in spite of the changes made in 1985, questioning about sexual character and history remains common (Brown, Burman and Jamieson, *Sex Crimes on Trial* (1992)). The 1995 Act introduced no changes to the substantive law in the light of this report.

There are few reported cases on these provisions. In *Bremner v. H.M. Advocate* (1992), a rape case, the trial judge disallowed questioning about a relationship between the accused and the complainer which had ended some eight months prior to the incident. His decision was upheld on appeal, and although the High Court implied some reservations about the exclusion of the evidence in this case, they emphasised that the decision in such cases is very much a matter for the discretion of the trial judge and one which will not be reviewed except where the decision was not one which a reasonable judge could have made.

The accused

Evidence about the accused's character and previous convictions is also prohibited by the rule. The prohibition applies both to the Crown and to any other person accused in the same trial (*Slane v. H.M. Advocate* (1984)). Again, however, there are exceptions. Broadly speaking these cover those situations in which the accused puts his character in issue, either by leading evidence to show that he is of good character, or by attacking the character of another person involved in the trial. The rules are now contained mainly in the Criminal Procedure (Scotland) Act 1995:

- Sections 101 (solemn cases) and 166 (summary cases) state the fundamental rule that the accused's previous convictions must not be placed before the court prior to sentencing. Breach of the rule will in most cases provide grounds to have the trial diet deserted or a conviction quashed on appeal (see, e.g. *Cordiner v. H.M. Advocate* (1978); *Graham v. H.M. Advocate* (1983)). The prohibition has occasionally been relaxed in cases where there was no intentional breach of the rule, and the court forms the view that there was no resultant miscarriage of justice (*McCuaig v. H.M. Advocate* (1982)). However, even an unintentional breach of the rule may lead to an acquittal if the circumstances are sufficiently serious. Disclosure *is* permitted in any of the circumstances set out in sections 266(4) and 270 of the Act. It is also permitted under section 101 where it is necessary to do so in support of a substantive charge. Driving while disqualified and prison-breaking are the classic examples of this situation although even in such cases, if the previous convictions laid before the court go beyond what is strictly necessary to prove the charge, the section may again be breached. In *Mitchell v. Dean* (1979), for example, a breach occurred where the prosecution laid six previous convictions before the court in order to prove a charge of driving while disqualified. But the provision also covers some less obvious cases—in *Carberry v. H.M. Advocate* (1975), for example, the charge was one of conspiracy to rob a bank. The Crown were permitted to lead evidence disclosing that a car used in the robbery had been obtained by the accused from a man he had met a year earlier while they had both been in Barlinnie prison.

- Section 266—this restates as a general rule that the accused must not be asked and if asked is not obliged to answer any question "tending" to show that he is of bad character or has previous convictions. But, under this section, the accused *may* be cross-examined as to his character or convictions where:

  (a) proof that he has been convicted of an offence is admissible evidence in relation to the offence with which he is charged—as in the situations described in the previous paragraph;

  (b) the accused has given evidence against a co-accused in the same proceedings. Note that, in contrast to the following subsections, there is no discretion here to exclude character evidence against an accused who "infringes" under this subsection (*McCourtney v. H.M. Advocate* (1977));

  (c) the accused has placed his character in issue—by cross-examining prosecution witnesses either to establish his own good character, or to impugn the character of the complainer. (Note that this subsection does not cover the situation in which the accused leads evidence from his own witnesses on these matters.); or

  (d) the nature or conduct of the defence is such as to involve imputations on the character of the prosecutor, complainer or other

Crown witnesses. *Leggate v. H.M. Advocate* (1988) sets out the principles which govern this important exception. It used to be thought that where the conduct of a defence fairly and necessarily involved casting imputations on prosecution witnesses—such as an allegation that police officers conspired to "frame" the accused—then the "shield" provided by this section was not lost. Only where the imputations were cast maliciously, or purely to discredit Crown witnesses, would the accused be liable to cross-examination on his own character (see *O'Hara v. H.M. Advocate* (1948); *Templeton v. McLeod* (1985)). Following *Leggate*, in *any* case where imputations are cast upon a Crown witness, the accused becomes liable to cross-examination on his character. However, the prosecutor must in every case apply to the court for leave to conduct such a cross-examination, and the trial judge then has a discretion whether or not to allow it. In doing so, she may take into account those factors which were relevant under the previous law, such as the purpose for which the imputations were cast. Simply to accuse a witness of lying is not, however, to cast an imputation on his general character for the purposes of *Leggate*. If that were so, the shield of section 266 would be lost in almost every case. *Sinclair v. Macdonald* (1996) was a marginal case in which evidence as to character *was* allowed under the *Leggate* guidelines. In that case, the accused was charged with dangerous driving. The main Crown witness was the driver of the car which the accused was overtaking at the time of the alleged offence. The defence agent suggested not merely that she was lying in her account of the incident, but also that in fact she was to blame, because she had deliberately accelerated while the accused was overtaking in order to prevent him moving back on to the correct side of the road. This suggestion clearly crossed the line between merely testing the witness on the one hand, and casting imputations on the other.

• Section 270—This section permits the Crown to *lead* evidence of an accused's character where the accused has himself led evidence of his own good character, impugning the character of Crown witnesses, or where, as under section 266, the nature and conduct of the defence is such as to cast imputations on the character of the prosecutor, complainer, or other prosecution witnesses. The section was a necessary addition to the 1995 Act, since, if the accused did not himself give evidence, then obviously there was no way that he could be asked in cross-examination about his character or previous convictions. In relation to this last proviso, the rules laid down in *Leggate v. H.M. Advocate*, and discussed above, once again apply.

V. OPINION EVIDENCE

The general rule is that opinion evidence is inadmissible. However, in a system which tends towards a fairly liberal approach to the admission of evidence, this rule is applied perhaps with particular laxity. One obvious reason for this is that it is rather difficult to distinguish between evidence of fact (which, of course, is allowed) and evidence of opinion (which, in theory, is not). As Walker and Walker pointed out: "Testimony which at first sight appears to be of fact, may prove to be actually of belief or opinion. Identification of a person is one instance … This may range from 'that is my partner' to 'that is the stranger I saw in the close that night'." In practice, therefore, lay witnesses may often be asked to express an opinion or to tell the court what impressions they formed at the time of a particular incident. Walker and Walker give some examples: in an action for divorce on the grounds of adultery, a person who entered the room where the act allegedly took place was allowed to give evidence as to the impression she formed when she saw the "position" of the defender and the paramour; a police officer was allowed to express an opinion as to whether a hole in the pavement was dangerous; and lay witnesses have been allowed to give an opinion as to whether handwriting was that of a particular person or whether a particular substance was or was not cannabis resin.

The "ultimate issue" rule

It does appear to be settled, however, that a witness, whether lay or expert, should not be allowed to express an opinion as to whether the facts in issue have been made out—that is, on the very issue or issues to be decided by the court. This is sometimes described as the "ultimate issue" rule. For example, a witness might give evidence in a criminal trial as to the speed at which a car was travelling shortly before a collision—evidence which, once again, is clearly the expression of an opinion—but will not generally be permitted to say whether, in his opinion, the accused was driving recklessly or carelessly, that being the issue on which the court must rule. In *Hendry v. H.M. Advocate* (1987), a culpable homicide case, the main point of dispute was whether a minor assault on an elderly man had caused him to have a fatal heart attack. Medical witnesses were permitted to give an opinion as to the factors which might have caused such an attack, and as to the possible causal link between the stress caused by the assault and the victim's death. They were not permitted to say whether they thought that the link was established "beyond reasonable doubt" since that would usurp the fact-finding function of the jury. Again, in *Ingram v. Macari* (1983), the rule was applied to exclude evidence from a psychologist as to the tendency of pornographic magazines to deprave and corrupt their readers, since, in the context of a case which turned on the alleged indecency of the publications, that was a matter for the sheriff to decide.

Expert opinion evidence

Much of the point of having a jury to find the facts rests in their (alleged) ability to apply their own common sense and experience of life in order to determine whether the parties have discharged their respective burdens of proof. The same applies where a judge is the fact-finder. However, where the subject-matter of the case is of a scientific, medical or technical nature, common sense may not be sufficient since the evidence may involve matters about which the fact-finders have no experience or knowledge. In such cases, an expert may be called both to give factual evidence on the technical matters involved, and to express an opinion about the effect of such evidence. Such an opinion is not regarded as decisive or binding, however, and the role of deciding upon the facts remains firmly that of the court. In *Davie v. Magistrates of Edinburgh* (1953), Lord President Cooper said that:

> "Expert witnesses, however skilled or eminent, can give no more than evidence. They cannot usurp the functions of the jury or Judge sitting as a jury, any more than a technical assessor can substitute his advice for the judgment of the Court …Their duty is to furnish the Judge or jury with the necessary criteria for testing the accuracy of their conclusions, so as to enable the Judge or jury to form their own independent judgment by the application of these criteria to the facts proved in evidence. The scientific opinion evidence, if intelligible, convincing and tested, becomes a factor (and often an important factor) for consideration along with the whole other evidence in the case, but the decision is for the Judge or jury. In particular, the bare *ipse dixit* of a scientist, however eminent, upon the issue in controversy, will normally carry little weight, for it cannot be tested by cross-examination nor independently appraised, and the parties have invoked the decision of a judicial tribunal and not an oracular pronouncement by an expert".

One implication of this is that an expert's opinion is not to be regarded as sacrosanct, and it is perfectly competent not only for a trial judge to decline to follow the opinion of an expert, but also for an appeal court to take a different view of the expert's evidence from that of the trial judge (provided, of course, there is evidence upon which to found such a differing approach— see *Stephen v. Scottish Boatowners Mutual Insurance Association*, (1989)).

An obligation to lead expert evidence?

In most cases it will be obvious that technical assistance is required. A jury unassisted by a medical expert is unlikely to be able to interpret complex evidence about diagnosis, treatment and prognosis in cases involving industrial injury or disease, for example. Again, where it is said that a person was mentally ill at the time of an offence, then clearly evidence from a psychiatrist will be admissible as to that illness or condition—indeed, in such cases medical or psychiatric evidence would normally be regarded as essential. There will be borderline cases, however, where lay evidence may be admitted on issues which, on one view, could be described as technical ones. In *Kenny v. Tudhope* (1984), police officers were permitted to give evidence that the accused's breath smelled of alcohol, his speech slurred and his eyes glazed, where the charge was one of driving while unfit to do so through the use of drink or drugs. It can be seen, however, that in this example the issue is one upon which most adults could be expected to form a reasonably reliable view, given an awareness of the everyday use and abuse of alcohol, and its effects. The same cannot be said for less commonplace occurrences and conditions, however, and whether expert evidence should be admitted is ultimately a matter of law. It is a matter upon which there is room for considerable disagreement, since different judges may take different views as to the extent of the common knowledge and experience of a jury.

Expert psychological evidence

For example, difficulties have arisen, at least in England, as to the admissibility of expert psychological evidence as to the mental characteristics of an accused person or a witness falling short of insanity. In *R. v. Turner* (1975), it was held, in a logical extension of the principle in *Davie v. Magistrates of Edinburgh*, that expert evidence which relates to some matter deemed to be within the knowledge and experience of the jury is inadmissible. The court went on to say that matters of human nature and behaviour, within the limits of normality, are matters on which a jury is competent to decide without assistance. The difficulty with this view lies, of course, in deciding which conditions or behaviours are "normal" and which "abnormal". The English Court of Appeal initially took the view that clinically demonstrable mental illness should be taken as representing the borderline. In practice this meant that accused persons suffering from personality disorders, or who were abnormally "suggestible"—that is, vulnerable to pressure or persuasion by an interrogator—were unable to lead expert evidence to show that their confessions may have been unreliable. Since they were not regarded as being mentally ill, the jury was deemed to be competent to interpret evidence about their behaviour without expert psychological assistance (see, for example, the cases of *Masih* (1986), *Weightman* (1991), and *Roberts* (1990)). The Court of Appeal has now adopted a more liberal position in this regard, however, and the cases of *Raghip* (1991), and *Ward* (1993), indicate that expert evidence will be admitted if it is thought likely to be of assistance to the jury in assessing the mental condition of an accused person. It should be noted, however, that this approach applies only where disputed confession evidence is concerned. Such evidence remains inadmissible in relation to issues of *mens rea* unless, once again, there is some suggestion of actual mental illness.

Scotland has seen little of this controversy. The recent case of *Blagojevic v. H.M. Advocate* (1995) implies that provided a proper evidential foundation is laid beforehand, psychological evidence about the "suggestibility" of an accused person may properly be admitted. Again, in *Lockhart v. Stainbridge* (1989), evidence from a psychologist was admitted in relation to the accused's fear of needles. It seems likely, however, that the Scottish courts would follow the *Turner* case in relation to matters of *mens rea*, given that in Scotland diminished responsibility requires proof of a mental illness or disease—that is, a condition clearly *beyond* the bounds of "normality".

Establishing the expert's qualifications

In general it is necessary to establish that an expert witness is properly (and preferably well) qualified to give evidence about the matter in hand. The first questions asked of a medical witness, for example, will be about her studies, degrees, diplomas, research, publications, memberships of professional bodies such as the Royal College of Physicians or Surgeons, and experience in the field concerned. It will usually be a simple matter to establish the witness's expertise, given the need for formal qualifications in most scientific or technical fields. But it is not essential that the expert has such qualifications, provided that she can demonstrate some experience or has informally acquired expertise in the field (*Hopes and Lavery v. H.M. Advocate* (1960)). In *White v. H.M. Advocate* (1986), for example, experienced police officers were permitted to give evidence as to the amount of a drug which a user might possess for his own consumption, and in *R. v. Murphy* (1980) as to the speed and displacement of vehicles involved in a road accident. Again, in *Wilson v. H.M. Advocate* (1988), police officers in the Drugs Squad were allowed to disclose "received wisdom of persons concerned in drugs enforcement" garnered at seminars and in discussions with customs officers.

Once it has been established that a witness is an expert, she will not be confined rigidly to her own area of expertise (although a witness would be unwise to offer an opinion on a matter outwith that field), and will be permitted, in giving evidence, to refer to the published or unpublished work of others in her own or related fields, and to relevant official tables and formulae. Thus, in *Abadom* (1982), where a crucial issue was whether shards of glass found on the accused's shoes corresponded to glass broken at the scene of a robbery, an expert gave evidence based on statistics collected by the Home Office Central Research Establishment as to the frequency of occurrence of glass with a given refractive index. Again, in *Main v. Andrew Wormald Ltd* (1988), a chest specialist was permitted to refer to a work by an epidemiologist.

Establishing the factual basis for expert testimony

Before expert opinion evidence can competently be led, a factual basis for the expression of such opinions must be established. Thus, in *Blagojevic v. H.M. Advocate* (1995), a case in which the accused disputed the reliability of his confession, expert psychological evidence as to the accused's "suggestibility" was excluded on the technical ground that, since the accused had not himself given evidence as to the nature of his interrogation, there was no proper evidential foundation for expert evidence regarding the stress or pressure to which the accused had been subjected in police interviews.

The court declined on that basis to apply the English authorities on the admissibility of such evidence.

A slightly different type of problem arose in *Forrester v. H.M. Advocate* (1952). In that case the accused was charged with "safe-blowing"—theft by opening lockfast places by means of explosives. The evidence against him was entirely circumstantial and based on three main points: (1) that when the accused was arrested he was in possession of some bank notes stolen from the safe in question; (2) that a cut on one of his fingers matched that on a glove found near the scene; and (3) that a small particle of material found in one of his pockets corresponded with the material of a cotton bedspread used in connection with the crime. The accused was convicted and appealed successfully on the ground that the evidence had not properly established that the fragment of material, examined and identified by an expert witness as that used in the crime, was the piece of material found in the accused's pocket.

This particular situation is unlikely to recur, thanks to the Criminal Procedure (Scotland) Act 1995, s.68, which provides that:

> "it shall not be necessary to prove—(a) that [a] production was received by [the expert witness] in the condition in which it was taken possession of by the procurator fiscal or the police and returned by him after his examination of it to the procurator fiscal or the police; or (b) that the production examined by him is that taken possession of by the procurator fiscal or the police,"

unless specific objection is taken to the provenance of the production. *Forrester* nevertheless illustrates the need for attention to detail in the laying of an evidential foundation for expert opinion, in both civil and criminal cases.

Corroboration of expert testimony

In *Davie v. Magistrates of Edinburgh* (1953), it was suggested that expert witnesses do not require to be corroborated. That view should be treated with caution. It is now *partly* true as a result of the general abolition by the Civil Evidence (Scotland) Act 1988, s.1 of the need for corroboration in civil causes, and comments by Lord President Hope in *M v. Kennedy* (1993) certainly support the view that in such cases corroboration of expert witnesses is not only unnecessary but may in some cases be regarded with disfavour by the courts. Moreover, in certain types of civil actions, parties are restricted in the use of experts to such an extent that corroboration may in any event be impossible (see Rules of the Court of Session, rr. 43.18–43.28—"Optional Procedure in Certain Actions of Damages"). In criminal proceedings, however, it remains the case that expert evidence in relation to any fact in issue must be corroborated (see *Stair Memorial Encylopaedia*, Vol.10, para. 651(5) and compare *Hendry v. H.M. Advocate* (1987), above).

VI. JUDICIAL KNOWLEDGE, AGREEMENT AND ADMISSIONS

It is unnecessary, and usually incompetent, to lead evidence about matters which fall within judicial knowledge, or which have been the subject of agreement between the parties or of judicial admissions (*i.e.* admissions made in court or as part of the court process) by one or other of them.

Judicial knowledge

Where a fact can be "immediately ascertained from sources of indisputable accuracy", or is "so notorious as to be indisputable", the court will recognise the existence of that fact without requiring evidence to be led about it (see Walker and Walker). In *Donaldson v. Valentine* (1996), for example, the fact that the prefix "M" denotes a motorway was held to be within judicial knowledge. It is sometimes said that in these circumstances the court takes "judicial notice" of the fact.

- There are two categories of fact which may be classed as being within judicial knowledge. The first comprises facts which require to be verified by consulting recognised works of reference such as dictionaries, textbooks or almanacs. In *Commissioners of Inland Revenue v. Russell* (1955) , for example, the Inner House consulted Murray's *Oxford Dictionary* and the *Shorter Oxford English Dictionary* in order to ascertain the meaning of the words "stepson" and "stepdaughter". The second category contains those facts deemed to be within the general knowledge of the court without the need for recourse to any work of reference. Thus, the date on which Christmas Day falls, the fact that cats are quadrupeds, and that King James VI of Scotland was also James I of England, are all matters about which no evidence need be led.
- Judicial knowledge may vary according to both the circumstances and the location of the case being heard. Thus, the definition and purpose of certain fishing implements—cleeks, gaffs and rake hooks—were deemed in *Oliver v. Hislop* (1946) to be within the judicial knowledge of a Borders sheriff. Again, whether a road is one which a local authority has a duty to maintain may be within judicial knowledge in some cases— a motorway would be an obvious example—but not in others.
- However, a judge must not apply purely personal knowledge to a case before him; nor must he make findings in fact based on his own examination of the evidence. In *Kennedy v. Smith and Ansvar Insurance Ltd* (1976) it was held that the Lord Ordinary was not entitled to assume that a person unused to the consumption of alcohol would have been "under the influence of alcohol" after drinking a pint and a half of lager on an empty stomach. In *McCann v. Adair* (1951) a car-dealer's conviction for fraud was quashed after it was shown that the Sheriff's assessment of certain documents was made entirely on the basis of his own examination of them and not on the basis of any evidence led in the case. Again, in *Brims v. MacDonald* (1993), a sheriff conducted an inspection of the site of an accident on his own and outwith the presence of either the procurator fiscal or the defence agent. It was held that he

should not have proceeded to any extent on the basis of this independent inspection and the accused's conviction for dangerous driving was quashed.

- The law of Scotland is, in general, within the judicial knowledge of the Scottish courts. The terms and authority of the recognised case reports and of statutes need not be proved. Statutory instruments are probably also within judicial knowledge, provided they are properly made under powers granted by statute, but the matter is not entirely settled (see Field and Raitt, para.4.5). Byelaws and other government orders require proof (see *Stair Memorial Encyclopaedia*, Vol.10, para.511., *Herkes v. Dickie* (1958), *Donnelly v. Carmichael* (1996)), although *Valentine v. Macphail* (1986) suggests that certain government orders contain matter which becomes so well known that judicial notice can be taken of it. The judiciary must also take notice of E.C. law (European Communities Act 1972, ss.2 and 3). Foreign law, by contrast, is regarded as a question of fact about which expert evidence must generally be led (see *Kolbin and Sons v. Kinnear* (1930) and compare *Baird v. Mitchell* (1854)). English law falls into the category of foreign law for most purposes, although the House of Lords takes judicial notice of the law of all the United Kingdom jurisdictions (*Elliot v. Joicey* (1935)) and Scottish judges, bizarrely, must apply the English law of charity in income tax cases—*Inland Revenue v. Glasgow Police Athletic Association* (1953). In spite of all this, judges cannot realistically be expected to take judicial notice of the whole of the law, and accordingly it is the duty of solicitors or advocates to draw the attention of the court to *all* relevant authorities, whether favourable to their own case or not (see the comments of the Lord Chancellor (Birkenhead) in *The Glebe Sugar Refining Company v. The Trustees of the Port and Harbours of Greenock* (1921).

Admissions and agreement

Where the parties are able to agree particular facts, or where one party is prepared to admit certain facts, and the agreement or admission is made in the proper form, then once again evidence in relation to the matters concerned will be incompetent. Recent changes in both civil and criminal procedure have been designed to encourage agreement between the parties and restrict the extent to which the leading of evidence is necessary.

(a) Civil cases

Admissions made on record by a party to a civil case are generally conclusive against that party (*Lee v. NCB* (1955)). Admissions which have been validly deleted from the record—for example, during the adjustment of the pleadings—cannot, however, be founded upon (*Lennox v. NCB* (1955)). Mere averments in the pleadings, as Lord Sorn points out, require proof before any weight can be placed upon them, but if an averment is not specifically denied by a party, he may be taken to have admitted the point (see generally

R. Black, *An Introduction to Written Pleading* (Law Society of Scotland, 1982)). In *Binnie v. Rederij Theodoro B.V.* (1993), it was held that the phrase "believed to be true" in answer to an averment may be taken as an admission and no evidence need be led on that point. There is also a procedure (see the Sheriff Court Ordinary Cause Rules 1993, r. 29.14, and the Court of Session Rules, r. 28A.1) whereby a party may serve notice on another party, calling on the latter to admit specified facts. Failure to respond to such a call has the effect that the other party is deemed to admit the fact concerned.

Admissions may also be contained in a separate minute of admissions prepared by the parties and such admissions are, once again, usually conclusive. In *London and Edinburgh Shipping Co. v. The Admiralty* (1920), Lord Dundas said:

> "In this case the parties elected to renounce probation upon an agreed joint minute of admissions in fact. This course has its advantages, but also its risks. The adjustment of such a minute is, in my judgment, one of the most difficult and delicate tasks which fall to the lot of counsel. An unguarded admission, or an inadvertent omission, may be fatal. But, once adjusted, the minute forms the evidence in the case; it is the proof at large, in synthesis, and its statement of admitted facts must be accepted as final."

It seems, however, that in consistorial causes, any minute agreed by the parties may be reopened by the court and evidence led as to the matters contained in it (*Robson v. Robson* (1973)). This is principally because of the overriding duty of the court to oversee the welfare of the child. Again, it seems that admissions made orally in court may not bind the party making the admission (*Whyte v. Whyte* (1895)).

(b) Criminal cases

A plea of guilty is the equivalent of an admission on record in civil cases and is generally conclusive against the accused. It *may* be possible to withdraw a plea of guilty—for example, if the accused pleaded guilty while unrepresented (compare *Tudhope v. Cullen* (1982))—but this is impossible once sentence has been recorded. (In *MacNeill v. McGregor* (1975) it was suggested that a person who wishes to withdraw a guilty plea *might* be able to petition the *nobile officium* of the High Court in the absence of a remedy under normal procedure.) Where an accused pleads guilty to one of a number of charges, however, that plea should not be put before the court dealing with the remaining charges (*Walsh v. H.M. Advocate* (1961)). Even although an accused person pleads guilty, the Crown need not accept that plea and may lead evidence nevertheless (*Strathern v. Sloan* (1937)). This may be thought desirable in cases where there are aggravating or mitigating circumstances, and the practice of the Crown is never to accept a plea of guilty to a murder charge.

The accused may also be prepared to admit certain facts without pleading guilty—for example, where he or she admits that he performed the *actus reus* of the offence, but has a defence to the criminal charge, such as self-defence, insanity, or the consent of the complainer. As with civil cases, admissions and agreements may be made in separate minutes of agreement or admissions, and lodged with the clerk of court. Where such a document is lodged, it constitutes the evidence in the case in relation to those particular matters. Both prosecution and defence are now under an obligation to seek agreement on non-contentious matters in criminal cases (Criminal Procedure (Scotland) Act 1995, s.257). The duty imposed by section 257 exists only where the accused is represented. The onus is accordingly very much on his or her advisers to reach agreement with the Crown on matters considered to be uncontentious. No sanctions are provided in the Act for any failure to comply with the duty, although clearly it strengthens the hand of the Court in inquiring at an early stage in proceedings what steps have been taken by the parties to reach agreement. There was previously no duty to reach or even attempt to reach agreement on uncontroversial matters and the purpose of the section is obviously to expedite proceedings by disposing of such matters by agreement if possible. Section 258 provides a procedural mechanism whereby the duty imposed in section 257 can be discharged. Under that section a party to a criminal case may serve a notice on the other, calling on the latter to admit the matters referred to in the notice. Unless the other party challenges the notice within a set time period, the facts contained in the notice will be deemed to be proved without the need to lead evidence. Several other sections in the Act contain procedures whereby uncontentious or technical matters will be taken to be proved unless objected to (for example, in relation to scientific or forensic reports, and transcripts of taped interviews with a suspect—see *inter alia* sections 276, 277 and 282). These provisions are designed to speed up criminal proceedings and avoid the unnecessary leading of evidence.

VII. CONFIDENTIALITY AND PRIVILEGE

Once a legal action has been initiated, one party or another is entitled to seek recovery of documents, papers, records of conversations and other communications from the other party, in order to assist in the preparation of his case. The party seeking to recover documents prepares a list or "specification" of documents, then enrols a motion asking the court to approve the specification and to grant a commission and diligence for the recovery of the documents listed. Recovery of the documents specified is overseen by a "commissioner", usually an advocate or solicitor appointed by the court. The holder of the documents must usually produce the documents listed in the specification, but may object to their production on the ground that they are confidential or privileged. The categories of privileged communication are strictly limited, although Lord Sutherland's opinion in *W.P. v. Tayside Regional Council* (1989) suggests that there are no particular categories of claim for "public interest immunity" in Scotland, and that each claim will be considered on its merits (see below).

(a) Legal advisers

Communications between solicitor and client are privileged. In *McCowan v. Wright* (1852), Lord Wood said that: "The rule by which the communications between clients and their legal advisers are protected from discovery, is one of great value and importance, and, within its legitimate limits, ought to be strictly observed.

The rule is based on the idea that people should be free to discuss their legal problems and to seek advice without fear that their conversations or correspondence with their advisers will be used against them in court. The rule is not wholly inviolable, however, and correspondence between agent and client which discloses criminal or illegal conduct, such as an attempt to evade creditors, is not privileged (*McCowan v. Wright*, above). In general, the agent must have been in some way *involved* in the conduct, however, even if only as an innocent agent. In *Micosta S.A. v. Shetland Islands Council* (1983) a dispute arose over the extent to which the general principle of confidentiality could be breached. The case concerned an alleged abuse of power by the Council in refusing to allow a Greek registered tanker to dock and load oil at the Sullom Voe oil terminal. The Court refused to allow confidentiality to be breached in this case:

> "So far as we can discover from the authorities the only circumstances in which the general rule will be superseded are where fraud or some other illegal act is alleged against a party and where his law agent has been directly concerned in the carrying out of the very transaction which is the subject-matter of inquiry. In this case it is not suggested that the defenders' solicitors were involved at all in the intimation of the alleged threat by the harbour master and any confidential correspondence as to the defenders' views at the relevant time – for they were quite entitled to seek advice confidentially – clearly falls under the general rule ... There is no trace in authority of any relaxation of the general rule, where the law agent of the party accused of an illegal act has played no part in the act itself."

However, in *Conoco (U.K.) Ltd v. The Commercial Law Practice* (1997), the Court of Session ordered disclosure of the identity of a client where the client had sought to profit from a fraud perpetrated by another, and had communicated with the petitioners through his solicitors in order to do so. This was said to be a mere extension of the "fraud" exception mentioned in cases such as *McCowan* and *Micosta*.

There appears to be some doubt over the confidentiality of communications between a potential client and a solicitor who declines to act (*H.M. Advocate v. Davie* (1881)). Nor is it clear whether confidentiality applies to a lay representative, such as an advisor in a Citizens Advice Bureau, or to a solicitor who is acting in a non-professional capacity (see generally R. Black, "A Question of Confidence" (1982) 27 J.L.S.S. 299 and 389). Finally, it may be that legal professional privilege is lost in relation to child care proceedings (see the English case of *Re L* (1997)).

(b) Other professional relationships

Confidentiality certainly does not apply to every professional relationship. It does not apply, for example, to Marriage Guidance Counsellors (although

see the Civil Evidence (Family Mediation) (Scotland) Act 1995, s.1), nor
to doctors, bankers, accountants and other professional groups (*Stair
Memorial Encyclopaedia*, Vol.10, para. 686). Journalists are not usually
bound to disclose their sources of information, but under the Contempt of
Court Act 1981, s.10 there is a wide exception to this principle where it can
be established that disclosure is necessary in the interests of justice, national
security or the prevention of disorder or crime. In the unreported case of
Daniels (1960), it was held by Lord Patrick that a priest is not bound to
disclose matters revealed in the confessional (Joseph Beltrami, *The Defender*
(1988), p. 201; compare *Stair Memorial Encyclopaedia*, Vol.10, para. 685).
Neither does confidentiality apply to communications between family
members (*H.M. Advocate v. Parker* (1944)). The only exception to this rule
is in relation to communications between husband and wife, which *are*
privileged (Evidence (Scotland) Act 1853, s.3; Criminal Procedure
(Scotland) Act 1995, s.264(2)(b); and *Hunter v. H.M. Advocate* (1984)).
The privilege appears to apply to communications made during the
subsistence of the marriage, and is unaffected by the death or divorce of
the spouses. *Parker* emphasises that where information relates to the
commission of a crime, the only situations in which information is privileged
are where the information passes between solicitor and client, or husband
and wife.

(c) Privilege against self-incrimination

Subject to certain statutory exceptions (as to which see Chapter 8), no witness
can be compelled to answer questions the answers to which would be
incriminating of that witness (see *Livingstone v. Murrays* (1830); Dickson,
paras. 1786–1792). Similarly, questions which would implicate the witness
in the commission of adultery need not be answered (*Stair Memorial
Encyclopaedia*, Vol.10, para. 675). It would appear, however, that there is
no general rule that a witness may decline to answer questions which may
expose her to a civil action.

(d) Communications *post litem motam*

In very general terms, communications made with a view to litigation, or
where litigation is in prospect, are privileged. Older cases, such as *Admiralty v.
Aberdeen Steam Trawling and Fishing Co.* (1909), suggest that in order to
qualify for the privilege, a communication must be one made not "merely
after the summons has been raised, but after it is apparent that there is
going to be a litigious contention"; and in *Marks and Spencer v. British
Gas Corporation* (1983), Lord Hunter said that: "the contrast is between
reports which are designed to put the person concerned in possession of the
true facts, on the one hand, and reports made in contemplation of judicial
proceedings, on the other". Lord Hunter's approach to the question of
whether a particular report was made *post litem motam* was to examine a
number of factors including the purpose for which the report was written,
its general tone and content (these factors being relevant to the question as

to whether a litigious contest between the parties was then in view), the relative ease with which each party could obtain information; and generally the question of fairness as between the parties. While this may seem a sensible and a fair way to approach the question, it probably does not represent the present law, at least in relation to the most commonly disputed type of communication—reports or records of accidents at work. In *More v. Brown & Root Wimpey Highland Fabricators Ltd* (1983), the Inner House approved a line of authority which lays down the simple rule that reports and records of accidents, including photographs, prepared by or on behalf of one side are simply not recoverable under a specification of documents by the other side. The reason given for this principle is that "after an accident and even before any claim has been made, each party having a possible interest should be entitled to pursue his own investigations into the cause of the accident, free from the risk of having to reveal his information to the other side". Reports by employees present at the time of the accident and made to their employers at or about the time of the accident form an exception to this general rule, however, provided that the report is made as part of the employees' "routine duty", and without the opportunity for "too much reflection" (*Young v. NCB* (1957)).

(e) Negotiations for settlement or conciliation

In general, admissions or statements made during negotiations towards a settlement or in conciliation are inadmissible in any court proceedings. For example, the Civil Evidence (Family Mediation) (Scotland) Act 1995, s.1 renders inadmissible any information as to what occurred during sessions conducted by accredited family mediators. A number of exceptions to this rule are provided by section 2 of the Act. Similarly, communications with a conciliation officer in an industrial dispute are not admissible in proceedings before an industrial tribunal (Employment Protection (Consolidation) Act 1978, s.133(6)). Confidentiality may also extend to communications said to be made "without prejudice"—a common method of preserving the position of parties to a negotiation (*Bell v. Lothiansure Ltd* (1990)). However, the use of that phrase does not automatically confer immunity upon the communication or correspondence. In *Daks Simpson Group plc v. Kuiper* (1994) it was said that:

> "The general principle underlying the rule is that if offers, suggestions, concessions or whatever are made for the purposes of negotiating a settlement, these cannot be converted into admissions of fact. ... If, however, someone makes a clear and unequivocal admission or statement of fact, it is difficult to see what rights or pleas could be attached to such a statement or admission other perhaps than to deny the truth of the admission which was made. I see no objection in principle to a clear admission being used in subsequent proceedings, even though the communication in which it appears is stated to be without prejudice."

Thus, where a party makes a statement which is not "a hypothetical admission or concession for the purpose of securing a settlement but ... a simple statement of fact", then that statement will not be protected by using the words "without prejudice".

(f) Public interest immunity

Considerations of national security or overwhelming public interest may take precedence over the principle that disclosure of information may be necessary to the proper administration of justice. Thus, a litigant will usually be unable to recover documents which disclose high level government communications, or which deal with secret defence information. There is a distinction, however, between documents which are granted immunity simply because they belong to a certain class, and those for which immunity is claimed on the basis of their contents. In *Air Canada v. Secretary of State for Trade* (1983), for example, the House of Lords refused to order disclosure of certain ministerial policy documents on the grounds of "class" based public interest privilege. Where a communication is of a more routine nature, special reasons would have to be stated in order to obtain immunity (*Conway v. Rimmer* (1968)). The converse of this is that the courts will not automatically accept a Crown claim to confidentiality and may order disclosure in the face of a Ministerial claim to immunity (*Glasgow Corporation v. The Central Land Board* (1956)).

In Scotland, the view has been expressed that public interest immunity is of very limited scope. The case of *Higgins v. Burton* (1968) held that records of a "Child Guidance Clinic" were not covered by public interest immunity and could be recovered. Lord Avonside said:

"I would tend strongly to be of the opinion that there is no such thing as public interest in the sense in which that phrase is used in our Court unless the interest be a national one and put forward either by a Minister of the Crown or by the Lord Advocate. If the scope of such a claim was widened I can see no end to the repercussions which might arise and I would have thought that it should be strictly confined to the sources I have indicated. Even then, as is well-known, the courts in Scotland have always refused to be bound by a Minister's certificate, and its effect depends on the discretion of the Court."

It should be noted that claims to privilege by the Lord Advocate are not limited to governmental bodies only, but may extend to other branches of the executive. In *Friel, Petitioner* (1981), for example, the court refused to order disclosure of the name of a police informer, the potential risk to law enforcement being said to override the petitioner's right to pursue a claim for defamation. Moreover, while the Scottish view of public interest immunity, properly so-called, is a narrow one, claims to confidentiality based on a broader view of the "public interest" may be put forward by non-governmental bodies. In *A.B. v. Glasgow and West of Scotland Blood Transfusion Service* (1993), a person who had been infected with the HIV virus through the use of contaminated blood products sought to recover the records of the Blood Transfusion Service in order to make a claim against the person who had donated the blood. The Court refused to order disclosure, citing the potentially "appalling" consequences of a national deficiency in the supply of blood should donors be deterred from giving blood by a fear of breach of confidentiality. On the other hand, in *W.P. v. Tayside Regional Council* (1989), the Court granted a motion for recovery of records from the Social Work Department of the local authority. In that case a foster mother sued the Regional Council for damages having contracted Hepatitis B from a child whose natural mother was an intravenous drug user. She sought to recover records from the Council Social Work department in order to throw light upon the Council's state of knowledge as to the natural mother's health. Lord Sutherland held that in this case the public interest in seeing justice done far outweighed the public interest in favour of confidentiality. Thus, each case will be decided on its merits; there is no rigid distinction in Scots law between the Crown privilege in the traditional sense, and a claim for confidentiality based on some other strong ground:

> "What has to be balanced in every case is the breach of public interest against the interest that is seen in the need that impartial justice should be done in the courts of law and that a litigant who has a case to maintain should not be deprived of the means of its proper presentation by anything less than a weighty public reason. It is therefore apparent that each case will depend upon its own particular facts ... The ultimate position taken up by counsel for the respondents was that the law of Scotland recognises a claim for confidentiality if it is strong enough to outweigh any interest to favour recovery. I would agree with this proposition".

Finally, the considerations which apply to a civil case are likely to be very different to those applying to a criminal trial. In criminal cases, the public interest will always be in favour of disclosure (see Sir Richard Scott, *Report of the Inquiry in to the Export of Defence Equipment and Dual-use goods to Iraq and Related Prosecutions* (HMSO, London, 1996), Vol. 3.

VIII. *RES JUDICATA*

Parties may not litigate the same subject-matter twice. This fundamental idea is expressed in the doctrine of *res judicata*. Consideration of the doctrine probably belongs more appropriately to a work on procedure. (For a fuller treatment of the *res judicata* plea, see Field and Raitt, *Evidence* (2nd ed., W. Green, 1996), Chap. 5). The effect of a successful plea of *res judicata* is that, once again, it becomes neither necessary nor competent to lead evidence in relation to matters which have already been decided. The rule applies both to civil and criminal cases, and in the latter type of case operates as a plea in bar of trial. In the criminal context the plea is known as "tholed assize" ("thole" is a Scots word meaning to bear or to endure).

(a) Civil cases

A number of factors must be present before there can be a successful plea of *res judicata*:

Prior decree pronounced by a competent tribunal

There must already have been a decree pronounced by a competent court. In most cases it will be obvious that this requirement is satisfied. (There is now no doubt that decrees of the Sheriff court are recognised for this purpose in the Court of Session—*Murray v. Seath* (1939); *Hynds v. Hynds* (1966)). Decrees pronounced by an arbiter are also sufficient to found a plea of *res judicata* (*Farrans v. Roxburghe C. C.* (1969)). In theory the same is true of statutory tribunals, such as employment or social security tribunals. In practice, however, such tribunals will often have exclusive jurisdiction over the subject-matter concerned, which is therefore highly unlikely to come under consideration in any other forum.

Same parties

The *res judicata* plea is intended to prevent the same parties litigating the same issues over and over again. However, the law regards parties as being the same not only where the parties are physically or legally the same, but also where one of the parties to the subsequent action is legally *associated* with one of the parties in the earlier action. For example, a person who has been represented in a previous action by trustees or an agent cannot bring another action in a personal capacity (*Glasgow Shipowners v. Clyde Navigation Trustees* (1885)). The converse is also true. Thus, if a person is injured in a car crash and sues the wrongdoer in delict, that person's insurance company cannot subsequently sue the same wrongdoer on the same grounds in order to recover their outlays (see, *e.g. McPhee v. Heatherwick* (1977)).

Decree pronounced *in foro contentioso*

The prior case must have been litigated to the stage of obtaining decree. Moreover, it must have been obtained in a defended action, and not merely pronounced in the absence of the defender (see *McPhee v. Heatherwick* (1977)).

Same subject-matter

Very generally, parties may not litigate the same matter twice. However, a second action is not *res judicata* merely because it deals with the same set of facts. A party wishing to plead to found on this plea must answer the question "What was litigated and what was decided?", and show that the answers to those questions were identical in each case (*Grahame v. Secretary of State for Scotland* (1951)). In *Hynds v. Hynds* (1966), for example, a woman sued her husband for divorce on the grounds of his cruelty. She had previously brought an action for separation and aliment, based on the same grounds, and the defender pleaded *res judicata*. The plea was rejected, since although the facts in issue were identical in each action, the remedies sought and the potential outcomes of the litigations were different. In the former action the marriage was preserved; the latter resulted in its dissolution.

Same grounds of action

Many texts describe this requirement as the need for the same *media concludendi*. There is some confusion in the authorities as to exactly what this means. In *Glasgow and South Western Railway Co. v. Boyd and Forrest* (1918), Lord Shaw's definition of the phrase was "the reality and substance of the thing disputed between the parties". This definition overlaps with the "same subject-matter" requirement. Maxwell defined the *media concludendi* as "the grounds of action in fact and law" (*Practice of the Court of Session*, p.197) In practice, it seems that what is involved here is that the facts in issue in each case must be the same. *Hynds v. Hynds* (above) illustrates, however, that even in cases where this is so, a plea of *res judicata* will not be successful unless each action leads effectively to the same result or remedy.

(b) Criminal cases

Res judicata is a plea in bar of trial in criminal proceedings. An accused who has been tried on particular charges is said to have "tholed his assize" and cannot be subsequently retried on those charges. As with civil cases, however, the fact that a case involves the same facts in issue does not of itself act as a bar to subsequent proceedings. It is not unknown, for example, for a person who has been convicted of assault, to be re-indicted on charges of murder or culpable homicide where the victim subsequently dies as a result of the original attack (see, *e.g. Tees v. H.M. Advocate* (1994)). But the Crown cannot, without a material change in the circumstances, simply re-indict an accused on different charges arising out of the same conduct. However, charges of perjury do not fall foul of this rule. A person who is acquitted of a charge having given perjured evidence at his trial, is not immune from trial for perjury since the charges do not arise out of the same conduct as the original trial, but from the trial itself (see *H.M. Advocate v. Cairns* (1967)).

Private prosecutions

Prosecutions by private individuals are extremely rare in modern Scots practice. Where they do arise, they form a partial exception to the *res judicata* rule in criminal proceedings. Thus, a private prosecution is competent following upon a prosecution brought by the Crown, provided that the earlier proceedings were deserted *simpliciter* or abandoned by the Crown (see *H v. Sweeney* (1983)). Where a verdict has been reached in the case, whether as a result of trial or plea, no further criminal proceedings are possible against the accused (although a civil action may be competent—see below). The same is true where the *court* has deserted the trial *ex proprio motu* (*Mackenzie v. MacLean* (1981)).

(c) Civil and criminal cases

The fact that a person has been prosecuted in the criminal courts is no bar to a subsequent civil action based on the same conduct. This is true even where the accused has been acquitted of the criminal act charged. In the case of *Mullan v. Anderson* (1993) the defender had been tried and acquitted of murder. The family of the victim successfully sued the former accused in delict to obtain reparation for her death, in spite of the fact that their action inevitably amounted to a rehearing of the issues raised in the criminal proceedings. In such cases, of course, the parties are different, and an essential element of the plea missing. There is some authority that where a private prosecution has been brought, the prosecutor cannot subsequently sue the wrongdoer in damages (*Young v. Mitchell* (1874)). The facts of that case were somewhat special, however, and it may be doubted whether the plea could operate generally in such cases, since the remedy sought differs— the conviction of the offender of a crime in one, and an award of damages in delict in the other.

---

8. WITNESSES

Most people may be called as witnesses in court proceedings and indeed may be compelled to attend and to answer questions. There are exceptions to this, however, the most notable being that of the accused in criminal proceedings. There are also complications relating to those who are accused along with others in the same proceedings; those who give evidence as accomplices or *socii criminis*; and the spouses of accused persons and of parties in civil cases. Finally, this section considers some of the difficulties in relation to child witnesses, again with the emphasis on child witnesses in criminal proceedings.

(a) The accused

- The accused is neither a competent nor a compellable witness for the prosecution. He may, of course, give evidence on his own behalf if he so chooses (Criminal Procedure (Scotland) Act 1995, s.266). Cases such as *Todd v. H.M. Advocate* (1984), emphasise, however, that if he does so he may be asked any question in cross-examination, notwithstanding that the answer may be incriminating, either of himself or of anyone else.
- Where an accused exercises his right to remain silent at his trial, the judge or prosecutor may be permitted to comment upon that silence and to invite the jury to draw adverse inferences from it. However, comment must be made only sparingly and with restraint (*Scott v. H.M. Advocate* (1946)). In the case of *Stewart v. H.M. Advocate* (1980) the defence was that an important Crown witness was lying, and the trial judge commented upon the accused's failure to give evidence contradicting that witness. The comment was held to be competent in the circumstances. The High Court noted, however, that:

    "This is a particularly delicate area in which comment has necessarily to be considered carefully lest a jury should receive the erroneous impression that they are entitled to treat the fact that the accused has not entered the witness box as a piece of evidence corroborative of the case for the prosecution, or worse, a piece of evidence which is to be added to a body of evidence which would be insufficient to satisfy them that guilt had been established beyond reasonable doubt."

- An accused *may* be called as a witness for the prosecution where he has pleaded guilty to, or is acquitted of, all charges which remain before the court, or if the charges against him are dropped (1995 Act, s.266). Where an accused is called as a witness having pleaded guilty, he may be treated as a *socius criminis* (see below) and loses any right to refuse to answer questions tending to incriminate him of the charges libelled.

(b) Co-accused

- A co-accused is, like any accused person, neither competent nor compellable at the instance of the prosecution, except in the circumstances outlined above.
- A co-accused may competently be called as a witness by another accused (see 1995 Act, s.266(9), above), but cannot be compelled to give evidence.
- Alternatively, an accused person may cross-examine any co-accused who gives evidence on his own behalf—and may ask that co-accused any question in cross-examination, including questions designed to incriminate the co-accused. But one accused cannot both call a co-accused as a witness *and* cross-examine him when he gives evidence on his own behalf (1995 Act, s.266(9)).
- An accused who gives evidence *against* a co-accused loses his protection against questioning on his character and previous convictions by both the prosecution and any co-accused—see the 1995 Act, s.266(4)(c) and Chapter 7.
- Evidence elicited from a co-accused which incriminates another accused can be used as evidence *against* that accused (*Todd v. H.M. Advocate*, above).
- It is doubtful whether a person who gives evidence on behalf of a co-accused (and not on his own behalf) may be required to incriminate himself. This is because of the terms of the Criminal Procedure (Scotland) Act 1995, s.266(3) which provides that: "An accused who gives evidence *on his own behalf* in pursuance of this section may be asked any question in cross-examination notwithstanding that it would tend to incriminate him *as to the offence charged*" [emphasis added].
- It is also doubtful whether the accused may be asked questions regarding criminal conduct not libelled in the indictment, although there is no doubt that the Crown can *lead* evidence of such conduct—see *Nelson v. Nelson* (1994) in Chapter 7.
- Where an accused does give evidence for or against a co-accused, he

should not be treated as an accomplice—see *Slowey v. H.M. Advocate* (1965), and *Casey v. H.M. Advocate* (1993), below.

(c) Accomplices

- A *socius criminis*, or accomplice, is a person who gives evidence for the Crown on the basis that he admits playing a part in the offence. Lord Keith said in *Wallace v. H.M. Advocate* (1952):

    "I am not satisfied that any witness can be treated as a *socius* unless he had already been convicted of the crime which is charged against an accused or is charged along with an accused or gives evidence in the witness-box confessedly as an accomplice in the crime charged. In all these three cases I think a witness is a *socius*. In the case of any other witness I should, as at present advised, hesitate to say that the court has any duty or right to arrogate to itself the task of saying that such a witness, who after all is not on trial, is a *socius* in the offence with which an accused is charged."

- A co-accused is *not* generally to be regarded as a *socius criminis*—see *Slowey v. H.M. Advocate* (1965), and *Casey v. H.M. Advocate* (1993)—but with that exception, Lord Keith's dictum seems consistent with the present law.

- A *socius* has no privilege in respect of self-incrimination and must answer all questions put by prosecution or defence. In return, the *socius* (provided he has not already pleaded guilty or been convicted) receives immunity from prosecution in relation to the offence about which he gives evidence. That immunity is, however, strictly confined to the libel in support of which he gives evidence. In *McGinley and Dowds v. MacLeod* (1963), three men were involved in a brawl which lasted a few minutes, beginning in one street, and ending in another. A was charged with assaulting B in the first street with a bottle, and B and C were charged with assaulting A in both streets by kicking him. B and C were adduced as Crown witnesses at the trial of A, who was acquitted. On the same day, the trial of B and C took place, conducted by a different depute procurator-fiscal and before a different sheriff-substitute. B and C were convicted. They appealed on the ground that, having given evidence for the Crown in the trial of A, they were exempt from prosecution in regard to the matter concerned in the trial of A. The appeal was refused, and their convictions upheld, the court holding that the exemption from prosecution only applied to a *socius criminis* and only covered the libel in support of which he was called to give evidence. The two accused were not accomplices of the third man, said the court, but "antagonists mutually accusing each other"; moreover, they had not all participated in the same crime, but had perpetrated separate assaults at different places. This case has been criticised as leading to an unfair result, since, having been called as Crown witnesses in the previous case, the accused had been effectively compelled to give evidence about the incident in which they were themselves implicated. Nevertheless, the decision was specifically upheld in the later case of *O'Neill v. Wilson* (1983).

(d) Spouses

• The spouse of an accused person may be called as a witness by any of the parties to a criminal trial (Criminal Procedure (Scotland) Act 1995, s.264). Section 264(2)(a) makes clear that he or she cannot be compelled to give evidence for the Crown or any co-accused. From this it follows, however, that the spouse *can* be compelled to give evidence by the accused spouse (see *Hunter v. H.M. Advocate* (1984)). The rules on the competence and compellability of spouses apply only to those who are legally married, and not to those in other intimate relationships, such as unmarried cohabitants (*Casey v. H.M. Advocate* (1993)).

• Broadly, the common law exception applies where the spouse was the victim of the offence. Such cases will generally involve assaults against the spouse, but in order to invoke the exception, there is no need to show that the offence was a violent one. In *Foster v. H.M. Advocate* (1932), for example, the accused forged her husband's signature on a number of cheques and uttered them as genuine. The husband's evidence for the Crown was held to be admissible.

• Having been warned that she is not compellable, a spouse who chooses to give evidence for the Crown or a co-accused must answer all questions put to her, regardless of whether the answers would tend to incriminate the accused (*Bates v. H.M. Advocate* (1989)). She need not, in common with other witnesses, answer questions the answers to which would tend to incriminate *her*.

• In any case there is an absolute privilege in respect of communications passing between the spouses during the marriage (1995 Act, s.264(2)(b)).

Civil cases

The competence of spouses as witnesses is dealt with by section 3 of the Evidence (Scotland) Act 1853. It is generally accepted that that section renders the spouse of a party a compellable as well as a competent witness in civil proceedings in Scotland. There is some doubt, however, as to whether a party to a consistorial action is compellable—cases such as *Bird v. Bird* (1931) and *White v. White* (1947) imply that the defender in such an action may refuse to give evidence, although the opinions delivered in those cases are critical of defenders who do so. (See Macphail on *Evidence*, para. 4.16 for a more detailed analysis of this point.) Finally, section three of the 1853 Act preserves the privilege in respect of marital communications.

(e) Children

In the old case of *Auld v. McBey* (1881) 18 S.L.R. 312, Lord President Inglis said: "I have found that when the question is as to what happened on a particular occasion the best witnesses are boys and girls. Their eyes are generally open and they are not thinking of other things and they are not talking to their neighbours". Although in England and certain other jurisdictions, children below a certain age are regarded as incompetent witnesses, it is accepted in Scotland that children of any age may be adduced as witnesses in criminal trials or civil proofs. Recent research suggests that children tend to be much more reliable witnesses than they have often (Lord President Inglis apart) been given credit for (see the survey in J.R. Spencer and R. Flin, *The Evidence of Children: the law and the psychology* (2nd ed., Blackstone Press, 1993), Chap. 13.

Competency

Much depends on the ability of individual children to communicate, and to communicate truthfully (although arguably this is or ought to be the major consideration in relation to all types of witness). Accordingly, one of the main issues for the courts in dealing with child witnesses is ensuring that the child is capable of giving intelligible testimony which is reasonably reliable.

- Criminal cases such as *Rees v. Lowe* (1989), *Kelly v. Docherty* (1991) and *Quinn v. Lees* (1994) make clear that before a child may be adduced as a witness, he must be examined by the presiding judge or sheriff as to his ability to do so and, in particular, his ability to differentiate between truth and falsehood. However, the rule also applies in civil cases, (*L v. L* (1996)). Such examinations will usually take place informally, in the judge's chambers. Failure by the judge to conduct such an examination will lead to the exclusion as incompetent of any evidence taken from the child witness. The rule has led to difficulties in relation to the admissibility of children's hearsay evidence in civil cases (see Chapter 9).
- *M v. Kennedy* (1993) makes clear that spontaneity—in the sense of an ability to give an account of a particular event—is not a matter which necessarily affects the question of competency. It is enough that the child knows the difference between truth and falsehood. In *M v. Kennedy*, a 12-year-old girl was referred to a children's hearing on the basis that she had been subjected to lewd and libidinous practices by her father. The parents did not accept the grounds for referral, and the matter was sent for proof to a sheriff. The child, meantime, had become an elective mute, and would answer questions only by nodding or shaking her head. It was accepted on appeal that an examination conducted by the sheriff on this basis was sufficient to establish the child's competence, in spite of the fact that she had to be comprehensively led through the

examination. Of course, the weight to be accorded to evidence in such circumstances might be thought to be negligible, but in children's hearing cases, it seems that the courts may be willing to proceed on the thinnest of evidence (see also *K v. Kennedy* (1992)).

• Extraneous evidence as to the truthfulness of child witnesses will usually be admissible. Thus, evidence from parents, foster parents, teachers or psychologists may be adduced on the question. Support for that view may be found in a number of recent cases, including *M v. Ferguson* (1994) and *K.P. v. H.M. Advocate* (1991), and in older cases such as *John Buchan* and *Malcolm Maclean* (1833).

Trauma

The other major difficulty which has exercised the law in recent years is the problem of the trauma caused to children and other vulnerable witnesses when giving evidence, particularly in cases where the witness has herself been the victim of the crime. In 1990, following publication of the Scottish Law Commission's *Report on the Evidence of Children and Other Potentially Vulnerable Witnesses* (Scot. Law Com. No. 125, 1990), Lord Justice General Hope issued a Memorandum on Child Witnesses. This gave instructions to courts about how to deal sympathetically with such witnesses—it recommended, among other measures, the removal of wigs and gowns by judge, counsel and solicitors; permitting a relative or other supportive person to sit with the child; and the clearing of the court of anyone not having a direct interest in the proceedings. A number of statutory provisions have also been passed to ameliorate such trauma:

• Law Reform (Miscellaneous Provisions) (Scotland) Act 1990, ss.56–59— introduced the possibility of giving evidence by live television link and specifically adopted the *ratio* of *Muldoon v. Herron* (1970) (see Chapter 7), to allow identification of the accused to be made by child witnesses in less stressful conditions than those obtaining during a trial.

• Prisoners and Criminal Proceedings (Scotland) Act 1993, ss.33–35— introduced further measures including the idea of giving videotaped evidence on commission and the use of screens to "shelter" the witness in court.

These measures were consolidated by the Criminal Procedure (Scotland) Act 1995 and are all now contained in section 271 of that Act. The Crime and Punishment (Scotland) Act 1997, s. 29, extends the protection of this section to other vulnerable witnesses, defined in the section as being those suffering from mental disorder or significant impairment of intelligence and social functioning. It remains to be seen whether this definition will cover, for example, adults traumatised by sexual or other assaults. While section 271 applies only to criminal proceedings, there is nothing to prevent a party in a civil case adducing as evidence statements contained in documents or on videotape, since hearsay is admissible in such cases as a result of the Civil Evidence (Scotland) Act 1988, s.2—provided, of course, that the witness meets the competency tests considered in the cases above. In terms of section 271, a witness may give evidence:

- On commission. The evidence is recorded on video and may then be played back to the court without the need for the child to attend. Where parties are authorised to proceed in such a way, the accused may not be present during the hearing.
- By live TV link. There are practical difficulties with this, and it appears that the court will by no means allow this procedure in every case in which a child has to give evidence. *Birkett v. H.M. Advocate* (1992) indicates that there must be specific averments about the trauma likely to be suffered by the child in giving evidence and about the reasons for it. It suggests that it is not enough merely to narrate that the *evidence* is of a traumatic or frightening nature; the child must have some reason to fear *giving* evidence in open court, such as a well-founded fear of the accused. Once a child has started to give evidence in this way, he or she cannot later be brought into court for examination or cross-examination, even in relation to crucial issues such as identification (*H.M. Advocate v. Brotherston* (1995)).
- From behind a screen to conceal the accused from the line of sight of the child while the child is present to give evidence.

Section 271(8) of the 1995 Act sets out a number of factors which the court may take into account in determining whether any of these measures should be taken. They include: the age and maturity of a child witness; the nature of the alleged offence; the nature of the evidence the witness may be called upon to give, and the relationship, if any, between the witness and the accused.

---

9. CIVIL EVIDENCE

In *Law of Evidence* Memo. No. 46, (1980), para A.03(5), the Scottish Law Commission stated as a guiding principle that the law of evidence in civil and criminal proceedings ought to be identical unless good reason could be shown for divergence. In fact, there *are* significant differences, and in a more recent report (on *Hearsay Evidence in Criminal Proceedings,* Scot. Law Com. No.149 (1995)) the Commission accepted (see para.2.12) that there are good reasons for applying different, and perhaps more stringent rules in criminal cases. The Civil Evidence (Scotland) Act 1988 certainly made far-reaching changes to the law, changes which take the law of civil evidence far from the law in criminal proceedings. For that reason it is appropriate to devote a separate section to the 1988 Act.

Corroboration

- Section 1 of the Civil Evidence (Scotland) Act 1988 abolishes the requirement for corroboration in all civil actions. Thus, the new rule applies to proceedings in "any of the ordinary courts of law", including hearings before a sheriff under section 42 of the Social Work (Scotland) Act 1968 to determine grounds for the referral of a child to the Children's Panel (except where it is alleged that the child concerned has himself committed an offence—*Harris v. F* (1991)); arbitrations; and proceedings for breach of interdict (*Byrne v. Ross* (1993)).

- In spite of the abolition of the corroboration requirement, civil courts will remain reluctant to find facts established in the absence of corroboration, and will exercise particular care in the assessment of uncorroborated evidence. Corroboration remains a "valuable check on the accuracy of a witness's evidence". (*Morrison v. J. Kelly & Sons* (1970); *McLaren v. Caldwell's Paper* (1973); *McCallum v. British Railways Board* (1989); *L v. L,* (1996), but compare comments by Lord Coulsfield in *L v. L* (1997)).

- There is authority (based on the provisions of the superseded Law Reform (Miscellaneous Provisions) (Scotland) Act 1968, s.9, which abolished corroboration in personal injury cases only) that, as a matter of law, a pursuer cannot succeed if corroborative evidence is available but without explanation not called (*Morrison v. J. Kelly*, above, and see *McArthur v. Organon Laboratories* (1982); *Sands v. George Waterston & Sons* (1989)). Section 1 is not so limited, however, and the courts appear to be moving towards the position that there is no such rule (see *McLaren v. Caldwell's Paper Mills*, above, and compare dicta of Lord Coulsfield and Lord President Hope in *L v. L* (1997), above, and *M v. Kennedy* (1993) respectively). It is certainly beyond doubt that no such rule exists in relation to proceedings under section 42 of the Social Work (Scotland) Act 1968 (children's hearings cases—see *K v. Kennedy* (1992)), although special considerations apply in such cases. It is probably also the case that a corroborative witness need not be called if he is being blamed for the incident leading to the pursuer's cause of action (*McLaren v. Caldwell's Paper Mills*, above).

- A pursuer may succeed in an action even although a corroborative witness is rejected as being unreliable (*Thomson v. Tough Ropes* (1978); *Comerford v. Strathclyde R. C.* (1987). Where there is a clear conflict between two witnesses who are accepted as credible and reliable, however, it is unlikely that a pursuer will succeed without corroboration of his version of events (*Morrison v. J. Kelly*, above).

- An uncorroborated pursuer may succeed even although a finding of contributory negligence is made against him (*Ward v. Upper Clyde Shipbuilders* (1973)).

Hearsay

- Section 2 of the 1988 Act abolishes the hearsay rule in respect of all civil proceedings. Under that section, a court may find any fact established, notwithstanding that the evidence in support of it is hearsay. Thus, under section 2, hearsay is admissible "testimonially", that is as evidence of the facts narrated in the statement. It was, of course, this use of hearsay which was specifically forbidden by the hearsay rule (see Chapter 7). Primary hearsay remains admissible under the new rules.

• A court has no discretion under the new provisions to exclude hearsay evidence (*Smith v. Alexander Baird* (1993); *McVinnie v. McVinnie* (1995); *Glaser v. Glaser* (1997)). Provided that the other requirements of section 2 are met, the court must at least *consider* the evidence. However, the *weight* placed on the evidence remains very much a matter for the discretion of the court. Thus, while it is theoretically possible that a case might be established on the basis of an uncorroborated hearsay statement, it is unlikely that a court would be willing to proceed on that basis (although again, children's hearing cases may provide an exception—see *K v. Kennedy* (1992)).

• Section 2 provides that "a statement made by a person otherwise than in the course of the proof shall be admissible as evidence of any matter contained in the statement of which direct oral evidence would be admissible". "Statement" is defined in section 9 of the Act as including "any representation (however made or expressed) of fact or opinion but [the definition] does not include a statement in a precognition". It has been held that the generality of section 2, taken together with section 9, is enough to abolish the best evidence rule in relation to civil proceedings (see Chapter 7). Accordingly, direct oral evidence takes no precedence, and hearsay is admissible even where the maker of the statement has given evidence on oath denying the truth of the earlier statement (*F v. Kennedy (No. 2)* (1992)). Moreover, this interpretation of section 2 leaves no room for the application of any rule similar to the *Morrison v. Kelly* "rule" referred to in relation to corroboration. The fact that a witness is available to give evidence, but is not called, is no bar to the admission of hearsay of that witness. The only apparent exception to this is in relation to child witnesses (see *L v. L* (1996), referred to below).

• The provisions allow a hearsay statement to be admitted only where "direct oral evidence by that person would be admissible". Thus, a statement to which privilege would have attached if tendered as evidence in court does not become admissible merely because of the provisions of section 2. Again, if a person would not have been a competent witness at a proof, then a hearsay statement from that person will not be admissible either. However, section 2 does not specify the time at which competency is to be judged. This creates difficulties where, for example, a witness was competent to give evidence at the time a statement was made, but has become incompetent by the date of the proof. There are dicta in the cases of *M v. Kennedy* (1993) and

M v. Ferguson (1994) which suggest that the relevant time to assess the question of competence (the *tempus inspiciendum*) is the time at which the statement was made. In the more recent case of *L v. L* (1996) it was held, however, that the *tempus inspiciendum* is the date of the proof. Thus a hearsay statement may be excluded, in spite of the fact that a witness was perfectly competent to give evidence at the time he made the statement. *L v. L* also holds that where the witness concerned is a child, that witness must be adduced at the proof and examined as to his competence before any hearsay statement made by that child can be admitted.

- Traditionally, precognitions have been excluded as being unreliable. In the criminal case of *Kerr v. H.M. Advocate* (1958), Lord Justice Clerk Thomson said that:

    "One reason why reference to precognition is frowned on is that in a precognition you cannot be sure that you are getting what the potential witness has to say in a pure and undefiled form. It is filtered through the mind of another, whose job is to put what he thinks the witness means into a form suitable for use in judicial proceedings. This process tends to colour the result. Precognoscers as a rule appear to be gifted with a measure of optimism which no amount of disillusionment can damp".

- Precognitions remain inadmissible under the 1988 Act (see the definition of "statement" in section 9, above). However, recent cases have distinguished between statements recorded as precognitions, which are excluded by the rule, and statements made to the precognoscer during or about the interview, which are not. In *William Anderson v. J.B. Fraser & Co. Ltd* (1992), for example, the court admitted evidence of statements made to a precognoscer during the precognition interview, but which were not recorded in the written account of the interview. A slightly different situation arose in *Highland Venison Market Ltd v. Allwild GmbH* (1992). In that case a precognition had been prepared and sent to the witness for approval. The witness revised the document, and returned it to the solicitor responsible for taking the precognition. The revised statement was admitted, since in revising it the witness had, as it were, reclaimed the statement as his own. Accordingly, it would appear that in such cases a statement will be admissible provided that the court is able to say that the statement is the unfiltered evidence of the witness, and not a version slanted by the precognoscer to favour one particular view of events.

- Statements made by children to social workers or others do not count as precognitions if the statements are taken with a view to proceedings under the children's hearing system (*F v. Kennedy (No. 2)* (1992)). This is because proceedings of that sort are not considered to be adversarial litigations in any ordinary sense.

Statements bearing on credibility

Section 3 of the 1988 Act provides that a hearsay statement is admissible in so far as it bears either favourably or unfavourably on the credibility of a witness. This modified the rule that evidence was not generally admissible where it was adduced purely to bolster credibility. Given the breadth of the rule in section 2, which provides for the general admissibility of hearsay for *any* purpose, it might be doubted whether section 3 serves any useful purpose. However, it was held in *Davies v. Maguire* (1995) that before a witness can be discredited (or presumably credited) by reference to an earlier statement, that witness must have given evidence in court. A statement cannot be led in advance of the witness's testimony to influence the court prior to the delivery of the oral evidence. Section 4 of the Act permits a party to recall a witness in order to discredit evidence using the provisions of section 3. In *L v. L* (1996), Lord Hamilton expressed the view that failure to call a witness capable of providing evidence in support of a witness who does give evidence in the case might lead the court to doubt the credibility of the latter. That view was doubted on appeal (*L v. L* (1997)). Thus, it seems that the only question for the court in such cases is the credibility and reliability of the witness who does testify.

Documentary evidence

While section 2 of the Act effectively abolishes the best evidence rule in relation to oral evidence, section 6 of the Act does the same for documentary evidence. Under section 6, copy documents are admissible as being equivalent to the originals, provided that the copy is authenticated by the person "responsible for making [it]". It is not entirely clear what is meant by this provision—in particular whether it is enough that the person who actually makes the copy should be the authenticator, or whether it is the person who instructs the copying who is "responsible". What is now clear, however, is that a copy must be authenticated before it is lodged as a production in a case (see *McIlveny v. Donald* (1995)) or at least before the time limit for lodging expires.

Further reading:

D.H. Sheldon, "Children's Evidence and the New Hearsay Provisions", 1997 S.L.T. (News) 1.

---

10. APPEALS

The basic rule

In both civil and criminal cases, appeals on the basis of purely factual matters are rare and are in any event unlikely to succeed. The reason for this is to be found in the importance attached by the adversarial system of procedure to oral evidence. Only the court of first instance sees and hears the witnesses, and has the opportunity to form a view as to their credibility and reliability.

An appeal court does not have that advantage, and so will be very slow to overturn the decision of the trial court, except where it is "satisfied that [the trial judge] has not taken proper advantage of his having seen and heard the witnesses" (*Thomas v. Thomas* (1947) *per* Lord Thankerton). Thus, an appeal on the evidence will succeed only if the reasons given by the trial judge for accepting or rejecting evidence are unsatisfactory, if "the [trial] judge has misapprehended the meaning of the evidence, or if it is clear that the evidence of a witness who has been accepted is clearly unreliable because it is inconsistent with itself or with other evidence" (*Macintosh v. NCB* (1988)). But it is "only ... on the rarest occasions, and in circumstances where the appellate court is convinced by the plainest considerations, that it would be justified in finding that the trial judge had formed a wrong opinion" (*McLaren v. Caldwell's Paper Mill* (1973)). Thus, before an appellate court can review the decision of the court of first instance on the facts, there must have been a patent error in the *assessment* of the evidence. In *Melon v. Hector Powe* (1980), Lord President Emslie said that:

> "The law is clear that where it cannot be shown that the tribunal of original jurisdiction has either misdirected itself in law, entertained the wrong issue, or proceeded upon a misapprehension or misconstruction of the evidence, or taken into account matters which were irrelevant to its decision, or has reached a decision so extravagant that no reasonable tribunal properly directing itself on the law could have arrived at, then its decision is not open to successful attack. It is of no consequence that the appellate tribunal or court would itself have reached a different conclusion on the evidence. If there is evidence to support the decision of the tribunal of first instance then in the absence of misdirection in law—which includes the tribunal's selection of the wrong question to answer—that is an end of the matter".

- The task of the appellate court is much easier where the dispute is as to the proper inferences to be drawn from the facts found, rather than about the particular facts which were found. In *Montgomerie & Co. v. Wallace-James* (1903), Lord Halsbury L.C. said that: "Where no question arises as to truthfulness, and where the question is as to the proper inferences to be drawn from truthful evidence, then the original tribunal is in no better position to decide than the judges of an appellate court".

- The abolition of the requirement for corroboration in civil cases (Civil Evidence (Scotland) Act 1988, s.1) does not affect the right and duty of an appellate court to examine, and if necessary to reverse, a trial judge's view of the facts (*Morrison v. J. Kelly and Sons* (1970)).

Fact and law
Difficulties have arisen over the classification of the matters forming the basis for the appeal as matters of fact or matters of law. The distinction is important because of the number of statutory provisions which render an

appeal competent only where the appeal is on a point of law. Appeals from sheriff court summary cause and small claims cases are in this category (Sheriff Courts (Scotland) Act 1971, s.38), as are prosecution appeals in summary criminal proceedings (Criminal Procedure (Scotland) Act 1995, s.175(3)), and appeals from a determination of an industrial tribunal (Employment Protection (Consolidation) Act 1978, s.136).

The distinction between questions of law and those of fact, however, is not an easy one to make. Many questions which have to be resolved by the courts involve a mixture of law and fact, and such questions have sometimes been called questions of *degree*. These in turn resolve into matters of fact which, as we have seen, are generally considered to be largely outwith the competence of appellate courts. *O'Kelly v. Trust House Forte* (1984), for example, concerned the dismissal of a number of people who worked for Trust House Forte hotels (THF) as "regular casuals". They were people who worked regularly—in some cases to the exclusion of all other work—for the company at banquets and other functions, but who had no formal contract of employment with THF. They applied to an industrial tribunal for a ruling that they had been unfairly dismissed. A preliminary question arose as to whether the applicants were employees or independent contractors—the relevant legislation applied only to employees. While acknowledging that the question whether someone is an employee or contractor is generally one of law, the Court of Appeal pointed out that the question involves consideration of a number of factors, and an examination of all the circumstances. Fox L.J. said:

> "In the present case the industrial tribunal in their full and careful reasons list nine circumstances which are consistent with the existence of a contract of employment, four which are not inconsistent with it and five of which are inconsistent with it. It seems to me that the case was indeed one where the answer, in the end, was a matter of degree and, therefore, of fact."

The Court accordingly refused to interfere with the decision of the tribunal.

Criminal cases

The Criminal Procedure (Scotland) Act 1995, s.106(3) (as amended by section 17(1) of the Crime and Punishment (Scotland) Act 1997) (section 175(5) of the 1995 Act is the equivalent provision for summary proceedings) provides *inter alia* that:

> "(3) By an appeal under subsection (1) above, a person may bring under review of the High Court any alleged miscarriage of justice which may include such a miscarriage based on—
> (a) subject to subsections (3A) to (3D) below, the existence and significance of evidence which was not heard at the original proceedings, and
> (b) the jury's having returned a verdict which no reasonable jury, properly directed, could have returned.

(3A) Evidence such as is mentioned in subsection (3)(a) above may
found an appeal only where there is a reasonable explanation of why
it was not so heard."

Thus, appeals on the basis of factual matters are generally competent,
provided that the lower court's assessment of the evidence is said to
have constituted a miscarriage of justice. Again, however, an appeal
court is likely to allow such an appeal only in the clearest of cases—
where the trial judge has materially misunderstood or misstated the effect
of the evidence (*Morton v. H.M. Advocate* (1938)) or where the verdict
of a jury is self-contradictory or perverse (*Hamilton v. H.M. Advocate*
(1938)).

Additional evidence

Section 106 formerly provided that an accused person could appeal on the
basis of fresh evidence, provided that such evidence "was not available and
could not reasonably have been made available at the trial...". This provision
was interpreted fairly restrictively. In *Salusbury-Hughes v. H.M. Advocate*
(1987) (a case decided under the identical section 228(2) of the Criminal
Procedure (Scotland) Act 1975, Lord Ross stated that:

> "Parliament has made it clear in section 228(2) that it is not enough
> to found an allegation of miscarriage of justice that additional evidence
> of a significant nature exists. To be the basis of an alleged miscarriage
> of justice it must be shown that the additional evidence which was
> not heard at the trial and was not available could not reasonably have
> been [made] available at the trial."

An attempt by Lord Justice General Hope to widen the interpretation of
the provision (in *Church v. H.M. Advocate* (1995)) was disapproved
two weeks later in the case of *Elliot v. H.M. Advocate* (1995). In *Church*,
a person was tried on indictment for assault and robbery. The robbery
was recorded on a video camera and evidence of the video film was
used by the Crown to identify the accused at his trial. Prior to the trial,
the accused's solicitor had instructed a consultant medical physicist to
conduct a comparison between photographs of the accused and the person
who appeared in the video film. The results of these comparisons were
inconclusive, but further comparisons were recommended. Such further
comparisons were not obtained, however, as the Scottish Legal Aid Board
would not provide the necessary funds. The accused was convicted, but
managed to raise the funds necessary for further comparisons to be made,
and these comparisons revealed inexplicable differences between the
accused and the robber. He appealed on the basis of this additional
evidence, arguing that the evidence could not reasonably have been made
available at the trial. The High Court held that section 228 (2) was wide
enough to allow the admission of the fresh evidence, since there was a
"reasonable explanation" for its non-production at the trial. In *Elliot*, a
Court of five judges led by Lord Justice Clerk Ross, overruled this
interpretation of the section, reverting to the traditional approach set
out in *Salusbury-Hughes* (above) and in *Beattie v. H.M. Advocate* (1995),

the latter case, oddly enough, being one decided principally by Lord Hope. The Crime and Punishment (Scotland) Act 1997 in turn overruled *Elliot* and gives Lord Hope's "reasonable explanation" test on statutory basis.

Section 27 of the 1997 Act also takes the rational step of creating a body called the Scottish Criminal Cases Review Commission. The purpose of this Commission, which is independent of the Crown, is to review cases in which miscarriages of justice are thought to have occured and to refer these, if appropriate, to the High Court for further consideration. It therefore constitutes a final "safety net" for those who allege that they have been wrongly convicted.

Further reading:

P. Ferguson, "Fresh Evidence Appeals" (1995) 40 J.L.S.S. 264.

Prentice, "Criminal Appeals" (1995) 40 J.L.S.S 469.

M. Scott, "Criminal Appeals and Additional Evidence—A Missed Opportunity", 1995 S.L.T. (News) 189.

D.H. Sheldon, "Additional Evidence and the Ancien Regime", 1995 J.R. 539.

W.A. Wilson, "A Note on Fact and Law" (1963) 26 M.L.R. 609.

W.A. Wilson, "Questions of Degree" (1969) 32 M.L.R. 361.

APPENDIX: SAMPLE EXAMINATION QUESTIONS AND ANSWER PLANS

1. "In R v. Kearley ... the question was whether the hearsay rule as known in England prevented evidence being led about requests for drugs made by callers on the telephone and in person, but in the presence and hearing of the defendant. It was held that the evidence, in so far as it might be used to imply that the defendant was a supplier of drugs, was excluded by the rule against hearsay, but Lord Griffiths and Lord Browne-Wilkinson dissented ... Lord Browne-Wilkinson's dissent was on the ground, which I think would cause no surprise in Scotland, that the evidence in question was direct evidence of a relevant fact, that is to say the existence of potential customers willing and anxious to purchase drugs at the premises of the defendant". (Lord Justice General Hope in Lord Advocate's Reference (No. 1 of 1992) (1992))

Comment on this obiter dictum, *referring, where appropriate, to English and Scottish case law.*

Model answer

This question concerns the distinction between primary and secondary hearsay, and the differing views taken in Scotland and England as to the scope of those terms.

Hearsay is evidence of a statement made other than in the course of a trial or proof. Traditionally, it has been excluded by the courts in both Scotland and England because it is not the best evidence, it is not given on oath and cannot be tested by cross-examination (see Lord Normand's dictum in *Teper v. R.*). However, the law distinguishes between two different types of hearsay. Essentially, the rule against hearsay forbids the use of hearsay statements as if they were the testimony of a witness given in court. This is what Lord Wilberforce meant when he referred in *Ratten v. R.* to the exclusion of hearsay when relied upon "testimonially". Hearsay in this sense is sometimes known as secondary hearsay. It is this use, and only this use of hearsay which is forbidden. In the recent case of *McLay v. H.M. Advocate*, for example, it was sought to lead evidence that a person other than the accused made a statement confessing to the crime charged. The maker of the alleged statement was not called as a witness. In these circumstances the statement was excluded as hearsay. It relied for its relevance upon the truth of the facts it narrated—in this case that the crime was committed by the maker of the statement. The statement was therefore being used "testimonially" and fell foul of the hearsay rule.

Where it is relevant to know simply that a statement was made at all, then evidence of that statement *is* admissible. This type of hearsay is sometimes known as primary hearsay. The making of the statement is itself *directly* relevant to the facts in issue. In *Ratten v. R.,* for example, the accused was said to have murdered his wife by shooting her. His defence was that the shooting was accidental. Evidence was admitted that shortly before the murder took place a telephone call was made from the victim's home. The caller was said to have been female, and in a distressed state. She asked the operator to connect her to the police. The making of the distressed telephone call in this case was directly relevant, since it tended to negative the defence of accident. Its relevance did not depend upon the "truth" or "falsity" of its contents.

Although both English and Scots law recognise the distinction between the two types of hearsay, it seems that English law takes a rather more limited view of the exception for primary hearsay. In particular it seems that in England the hearsay rule forbids the admission of any statement as evidence of any fact asserted *or implied* in the statement. The recent case of *Kearley* provides a graphic illustration of the breadth of this rule. In *Kearley*, the Crown sought to lead evidence of certain telephone calls and visits made to a house during a police search for controlled drugs. The callers had all asked for the appellant, "Chippie", and asked to be supplied with drugs. None of the telephone callers or visitors were called as witnesses, and the Crown sought instead to rely on police evidence of the calls. This was objected to as hearsay, an objection which the House of Lords ultimately sustained, Lords Griffiths and Browne-Wilkinson dissenting. The majority view was that evidence of the visits and telephone calls was relevant only in so far as it implied that Chippie was a drug dealer. The use of the calls as evidence of facts implied in them was said to infringe the hearsay rule.

In Scotland, by contrast, hearsay is inadmissible only in as much as a hearsay statement is relied upon to prove the truth of facts *asserted* by it. In

McLaren v. McLeod there was a charge of brothel-keeping. The prosecution sought to lead evidence of certain conversations overheard by police officers in the house concerned, in which female occupants of the house were heard to say that the accused had introduced "short time" to the house. This evidence was objected to as hearsay. The relevance of the statement in *McLaren* that the accused had introduced "short time" to the house could be explained only by reference to the fact *impliedly* asserted—that the women in the house were working girls. Whether or not the accused had in fact introduced "short time" to the house was wholly irrelevant to any issue in the case. Nevertheless, the hearsay statements were admitted as primary evidence that a certain type of conversation was taking place in the house. That fact in turn allowed the court to draw the inference that the place was being used a brothel. Following *Kearley*, it seems unlikely that such evidence would be admissible in an English trial. The Scots law of hearsay therefore seems to differ from the English view in that statements relevant because of *implied* assertions are not prohibited by the rule. This is borne out by Lord Justice General Hope's dictum in *Lord Advocate's Reference (No. 1 of 1992)* (1992), where he said that the dissenting opinions delivered in *Kearley* "would cause no surprise in Scotland [since] the evidence in question was *direct* evidence of a relevant fact, that is to say the existence of potential customers willing and anxious to purchase drugs at the premises from the defendant". It was just this argument which the majority in the House of Lords refused to accept in *Kearley*.

The law of hearsay in criminal cases has been the subject of recent reform (Criminal Justice (Scotland) Act 1995). Under the new provisions (now contained in the Criminal Procedure (Scotland) Act 1995) hearsay is now admissible in a wider range of circumstances than previously. The underlying principles remain unchanged, however, and it is notable that in their *Report on Hearsay in Criminal Cases* (1995), on which the new provisions are based, the Scottish Law Commission took the view that the law is as stated above, and that the hearsay rule in Scotland does not prohibit or attack facts implied in a statement, but only those which are expressly part of the statement.

2. Write notes on two of the following cases:

(a) Gillespie v. Macmillan (1957)—corroboration
(b) Muldoon v. Herron (1970)—previous identification
(c) Rhesa Shipping Company v. Edmunds ("The Popi M") (1985)—burden of proof.

Gillespie v. Macmillan

This case is widely regarded as having been wrongly decided. However, because of the conflict which arose in the case over two opposing theories of corroboration, it is important to understand where the High Court fell into error.

The facts of the case were as follows. The accused was prosecuted under the then existing road traffic legislation, the particular charge being one of speeding. To obtain evidence of the offence, the police set up a primitive "speed trap". They took an accurate measurement for a stretch of road, and positioned a police officer equipped with a stop-watch at each end of that measured stretch. When a car entered the "trap", the first officer started his watch; when the car left the "trap" the second officer started his. The watches would then be stopped simultaneously in the presence of the driver. The difference in the times was the time taken for the car to travel along the measured piece of road. The average speed of the car could then be calculated by dividing the measured distance by the time taken for a car to travel along it. The question arose as to whether there was sufficient evidence against the accused to obtain a conviction. In short, was the evidence corroborated?

The High Court held that in this case there *was* corroboration. All that was required, said the Court, was that there should be two witnesses to any criminal charge. Each fact in a criminal case could be proved by one witness only, provided that the facts formed a "consecutive chain" leading to the accused's guilt. In this case, it was thought, the evidence of each police officer formed just such a chain, leading inexorably to "one conclusion"—that the accused had broken the speed limit. It was, of course, the case that only one police officer spoke to each fact in the case.

This analysis obscures an important distinction, however—the distinction between crucial and evidential facts. Crucial facts are those which it is essential for the prosecutor in any case to prove. They will encompass the "ingredients" of the offence, such as *mens rea* and causation in a homicide case. In a criminal case, the crucial facts will always include the identity of the accused as the perpetrator and the fact that the crime was committed. Evidential or circumstantial facts, on the other hand, simply support the crucial facts. Unlike the crucial facts, failure to prove an evidential fact will not necessarily lead to failure in the case. Cases such as *Morton v. H.M. Advocate* suggest that each crucial fact requires to be corroborated, whereas evidential facts may be spoken to by one witness only. This view fits with the rationale behind the requirement for corroboration. Hume took the view that corroboration was required to prevent an accused person being convicted *on the strength* of a single witness's testimony, no matter how credible and reliable that witness might be. It has been argued—by W.A. Wilson, among others—that in *Gillespie v. Macmillan* the individual readings taken by the police officers were crucial to the case. After all, the case would inevitably fail if even one of those readings could not be proved. To allow a conviction on the basis that a single witness spoke to each of those readings was therefore to rest the whole case on the testimony of a single witness, which is just what Hume said must not be done. Accordingly, the testimony of the police officers in *Gillespie v. Macmillan* should have been corroborated, and the case was wrongly decided.

The Popi M

The Popi M was a ship which sank in a well charted shipping lane in the Mediterranean in clear skies and calm seas. The ship's owners sought to claim on their insurance policy in respect of the loss. The insurers disputed the claim. They contended that the ship had been lost simply because it was unseaworthy. In particular, they said that the hull of the vessel had been so badly maintained that even in calm conditions it had simply given way, thus holing the ship and causing the sinking. The shipowners sued the insurers under the policy. As plaintiffs the burden of proof rested on them to show that the policy covered them for the loss. The policy applied only where the ship was lost through the "ordinary perils of the sea", and so the plaintiffs had to prove that their ship had been lost because of such perils— the action of wind and wave, collision, and so on—and not merely because their ship was an ill-maintained rust-bucket. The insurance policy was void where the ship was unseaworthy. In order to bring themselves within the provisions of the policy, the plaintiffs put forward a number of hypotheses to explain the loss. These included collision with a submerged rock, with an unarmed torpedo, and with a submerged submarine travelling in the same direction and at roughly the same speed as the ship. The trial judge positively excluded all of these explanations except for that involving the submarine, an explanation which he himself admitted was "highly improbable". As the only remaining explanation, however, he felt constrained to accept that explanation and to find for the plaintiffs.

On appeal his decision was reversed. The Court of Appeal pointed out that Sherlock Holmes' famous dictum—"eliminate the impossible and whatever remains, however improbable, must be the truth"—has very limited application in the legal process. The trial judge in this case had failed to appreciate that there was another option open to him—simply to find that the plaintiffs had failed to prove their case. The persuasive burden lay on the plaintiffs—that is, they had to prove on a balance of probabilities that the ship had been lost through the ordinary perils of the sea. They had put forward a number of possible explanations, but there was very little hard evidence in support of any of them, except for what might in a criminal case be called evidence of opportunity. On the facts admitted or proved, the trial judge himself had taken the view that the submarine theory was highly improbable. Accordingly, it could hardly be said that the case had been proved on a balance of probabilities. The plaintiffs' case failed, since they had simply failed to discharge their persuasive burden of proof.

3. *Robbie is suspected by the police of involvement in a number of violent sexual assaults, all on prostitutes. In an attempt to obtain evidence to confirm their suspicions, a female plain-clothes police officer, Jan, is instructed to make contact with Robbie, and to befriend him, without revealing the fact that she is a police officer. Jan discovers that Robbie is registered with a dating agency and manages to arrange a meeting with him through this agency. She gains his trust, and they start to meet on a regular basis. During one of their meetings, she says to him, still without revealing her true identity, "Look, I know you were involved in those attacks. But don't worry—actually I think it's a bit of a turn on. Why don't you tell me all about it?" Robbie replies, "Yeah it was me that did a' they tarts". This statement is recorded by means of a radio transmitter concealed in Jan's clothing.*
(a) Is Robbie's statement admissible?

(b) The statement is the only piece of evidence against Robbie. Assuming that it is admissible, is there sufficient evidence to sustain a conviction against him?

Model answer

(*a*) Robbie's statement is probably *not* admissible. The basic test for the admissibility of incriminating statements in Scots law is that of fairness. This test was formerly judged purely by reference to the question of fairness to the accused but, following the case of *Miln v. Cullen*, is now a bilateral test. Thus, the court can take into account considerations of fairness to the public as well as fairness to the accused. The fairness test is, of course, a very broad one. It is accordingly necessary to examine the case law to determine whether the evidence gathered by Jan will be admissible.

There are no Scottish cases which are directly in point. In the English case of *Stagg*, it was held that evidence obtained in such circumstances is inadmissible. It is submitted that the Scottish courts would take a similar view. Although the over-arching test is one of fairness, there are strong indications in the case law that that test includes considerations of voluntariness. Thus, if evidence is obtained by means of threats, violence or other inducements, it may well be excluded. *Codona*, for example, was a case involving sustained and intensive questioning of a 14-year-old girl. Although there was no suggestion in that case of third-degree methods, the girl's confession was ruled to be inadmissible, the High Court emphasising the question of voluntariness. Again, if threats are made that a suspect will be kept in prison should he fail to confess, any statement is likely to be excluded on the ground that it was not made freely and voluntarily (*Black v. Annan*). Moreover, there are a number of cases in which statements have been excluded because they were given in the context of a covert operation of some sort. In *H.M. Advocate v. Campbell*, for example, a murder suspect made an incriminating statement to a reporter who was accompanied by a plain clothes police officer. The suspect took the officer to be another reporter. The statement was excluded. Again, in *H.M. Advocate v. Graham* the accused made a statement to a business associate who had been fitted with a "bug", and the statement was recorded by the police. Again, the statement was excluded. Doubts were expressed about *Campbell* by Lord Ross in the case of *Weir v. Jessop*, on the grounds that the statement was made voluntarily and without the exertion of any pressure on the suspect. Those comments were *obiter*, however, and both *Campbell* and *Graham* remain good law. In any event, the present case is at least one step removed from those cases. In this case, not only is there a covert operation by the police which leads to a statement being obtained and recorded, but there is also an apparent inducement by the police officer, Jan, to make the statement. The inducement is admittedly a fairly vague one, but the implication of possible sexual favours does appear to be there. It appears to have been that aspect of the case which led the court in the similar English case of *R. v. Stagg* to exclude the confession made. In this case it is arguable not only that the proceedings as a whole are unfair to the accused, but also that the statement may have been made in answer to the inducement made by Jan and was not wholly a voluntary one. Accordingly, it is submitted that the statement is not admissible.

(*b*) On the assumption that the statement *is* admissible, it is arguable that there is still insufficient evidence in law to obtain a conviction. While Robbie's reply to Jan's question or statement about the assaults may qualify as a "special knowledge" confession, it is submitted that since the confession is itself uncorroborated, a conviction cannot be obtained.

"Special knowledge" confessions form an exception to the rule requiring corroboration. Where a confession contains detailed information about the commission of a crime, and that information can be independently confirmed, then provided the court is satisfied that the accused knows the information because he is the perpetrator, the confession effectively corroborates itself. The leading case on self-corroborating confessions is the case of *Manuel v. H.M. Advocate*. In that case, the accused confessed to a number of murders and subsequently led the police to a place where various items belonging to one of the victims had been hidden. The discovery of this evidence, as a result of the information provided by the confession, was held to provide corroboration of the statement. This was, however, information which the police did not previously possess. In Robbie's case, it is clear that the police are already aware of the assaults. As the "doctrine" has developed, it seems that there is no need for the accused to tell the police anything new in his confession. The information provided may be to some extent within public knowledge (*Wilson v. H.M. Advocate*), and need not even be wholly accurate (*Gilmour v. H.M. Advocate*). The only test is that the jury should be satisfied that the accused possessed the information because he was the perpetrator. Robbie's statement in this case demonstrates very limited knowledge of the crimes, which would presumably be to some extent in the public arena. However, the case of *McDonald v. H.M. Advocate* shows that a very scanty "special" knowledge may be enough for corroboration. In that case, the accused made a statement during questioning referring to a particular armed robbery that he "did that one with Kenny and Bruce". Given that there were two co-accused called Kenny and Bruce, this was accepted as demonstrating special knowledge. In *Low v. H.M. Advocate*, on the other hand, a statement to the effect that the victim of a stabbing was to be found "lying in a pool of blood" was held to be insufficient for self-corroboration. Clearly the present case is on the margins of acceptability, and it might well be a jury question whether they were prepared to accept the statement as self-corroborating. However, it has been held (in *Mitchell v. H.M. Advocate*) that where the Crown relies upon a single confession as being self-corroborating, the confession must itself be spoken to by two witnesses—for example, two police officers conducting an interview with the accused. In this case, only Jan could speak to the confession. Accordingly, the requirement of *Mitchell* cannot be satisfied, and there would be insufficient evidence in law.

4. It has been said with regard to the Civil Evidence (Scotland) Act 1988, that "the effect of sections 2 and 9 taken together is that the best evidence rule is overridden". (Lord Justice Clerk Ross in F v. Kennedy (No.2) (1992)).

What are the implications of Lord Ross's dictum? Compare Lord Ross's approach to section 2 with the approach (or likely approach) of the Scottish courts to section 1 of the same Act.

Model answer

Section 2 of the Civil Evidence (Scotland) Act 1988 provides that any fact in a civil action may be found to be established notwithstanding that the evidence in support of that fact consists of hearsay. It goes on to provide that any statement made otherwise than in the course of a proof shall be admissible as evidence of any matter contained in the statement of which direct oral evidence by that witness would be admissible. Thus, hearsay is admissible "testimonially" in civil cases—that is, any hearsay statement is treated as if it were the evidence of a witness giving evidence in court. Section 9 is the definition section of the Act. The crucial definition is that of "statement" which is said to include any representation of fact or opinion, however it is expressed, but excluding precognitions. There is thus a very wide scope for the admission of hearsay in civil matters. Indeed, it has been held that there is no discretion to exclude hearsay provided that it meets the requirements laid down by sections 2 and 9 (*McVinnie v. McVinnie; Smith v. Alexander Baird; Glaser v. Glaser*). This is so even where a witness has actually given evidence in court, and even where the witness has denied the truth of the earlier statements. It was argued in *F v. Kennedy (No.2)* that in such circumstances the best evidence rule should operate to exclude the hearsay. The best evidence of that witness's testimony was what he said in court on oath or under admonition. Hearsay evidence was secondary evidence, was not given on oath, and could not be tested by cross-examination. On this argument, therefore, oral testimony in court would retain its traditional precedence over hearsay evidence. That argument was rejected by the Second Division. There are no qualifications to section 2 other than those set out in the Act itself. The court must take hearsay evidence into consideration even if there is "competing" oral evidence. The question of the weight to be accorded to the hearsay in such circumstances is another matter, and it may be that the court would be unwilling to place much reliance on hearsay in such cases. But, the court is entitled to consider it, and indeed to allow the hearsay evidence to override the oral testimony if that is considered appropriate.

This rather liberal approach may be contrasted with the attitude of the court to section 1 of the Act and its predecessor, section 9 of the Law Reform (Miscellaneous Provisions) (Scotland) Act 1968. The latter section abolished the rule requiring corroboration in personal injury cases only. The courts took a rather cautious view of the section and held that where a case was uncorroborated, special care was required in the assessment of the evidence and in making a finding in favour of the pursuer (see, *e.g. McLaren v. Caldwell's Paper Mills*). Some judges, notably Lord President Clyde, went so far as to suggest that where corroboration was available, but not led, then as a matter of law the pursuer simply could not succeed. The court could not be "satisfied" that the facts had been established in the absence of potentially corroborative evidence (*Morrison v. J. Kelly and Sons*).

Section 9 of the 1968 Act has been abolished and replaced by section 1 of the 1988 Act. The latter section abolishes the requirement for corroboration altogether in civil cases. While reference is still made to the 1968 Act cases, it would appear that the judiciary is moving away from the rather conservative approach of Lord Clyde. Recent dicta of Lord President Hope (in *M v. Kennedy*) and Lord Coulsfield (in *L v. L*) suggest that provided a witness is accepted as being credible and reliable, there is no rule that a failure to call corroborative witnesses bars success in the action. In relation to section 2, cases such as *McVinnie* and *F v. Kennedy (No. 2)* make clear that there is in any event no rule equivalent to the rule in *Morrison v. J. Kelly*. Even if a witness is available to give evidence and even if that witness in fact does give evidence, the court is not prevented from taking hearsay of that witness into account. Indeed, it seems that the court *must* at least consider that evidence. Thus, there is, historically at least, a difference in the approach of the court to sections 1 and 2 of the 1988 Act. It would appear, however, that any such distinctions are gradually disappearing, and that the court is becoming more willing to apply the bare terms of the legislation, rather than adding cautious riders of its own, as it appeared to do in relation to the abolition of the corroboration rule.

5. Outline the decision in McLay v. H.M. Advocate (1994) and explain how it has been affected by sections 17 and 19 of the Criminal Justice (Scotland) Act 1995.

Model answer
Hearsay is not generally admissible in Scottish criminal proceedings. Thus, evidence of any extra-judicial statement cannot be given in court unless it falls within one of the recognised exceptions to the hearsay rule (although it should be noted that the High Court has proved willing on occasion to create further exceptions to the rule—see, for example, *Lord Advocate's Reference (No. 1 of 1992)*). One exception to the rule is in relation to incriminating statements made by an accused person. Such statements *are* admissible, on the basis that since it is against the accused's interests to make such a statement, it is likely to be true or reliable.

Difficulties arose in *McLay* because a person other than the accused made a statement which incriminated him of the crime of which the accused had been convicted. Two men were tried together on a murder charge. Each lodged a special defence incriminating the other. McLay was convicted, and his co-accused, Harkins, was acquitted. McLay appealed against his conviction on the basis of fresh evidence, which was to the effect that Harkins had, both prior to and following his acquittal, made statements confessing that he was solely responsible for the killing. For obvious reasons, the co-accused was unwilling to give evidence at the appeal. For the appeal to have been successful, the High Court would therefore have had to have been persuaded to create a new exception to the hearsay rule, and this they declined to do. Arguably the extension to the rule sought in this case was less radical than the one which was permitted in the earlier case of *Lord Advocate's Reference (No. 1 of 1992)*. Nevertheless, the High Court felt that the danger of fabrication was too high in such circumstances, since a co-accused who has been acquitted cannot subsequently be re-tried on the basis of his later confessions, as a result of the *res judicata* rule, and they refused to extend the rule. The result seems somewhat unfair, since a confession made by an accused person clearly is admissible *against* that person. What *McLay* said was that such a confession is not admissible *in favour of* another person.

The extension to the hearsay rule created in *Lord Advocate's Reference (No. 1 of 1992)* was based on the idea that in some circumstances hearsay may be the best evidence available to a court. That case concerned the admissibility of computer records. Technically, such records are hearsay in the absence of witnesses who can speak to their creation. The court held that the records were admissible as an exception to the hearsay rule, given the impracticability of tracing and calling as witnesses the computer operatives who created the records. In the circumstances, the records were the best evidence available to the court. This idea was adopted by the Scottish Law Commission in their 1995 report on the admissibility of hearsay in criminal cases. The recommendations made in that report were incorporated into the Criminal Justice (Scotland) Act 1995, which was itself consolidated and incorporated into the Criminal Procedure (Scotland) Act 1995. The relevant provisions are in section 259 of the latter Act ("the 1995 Act").

The 1995 Act provides that evidence of a statement made otherwise than in the course of a trial or proof is admissible as evidence of the facts contained in the statement provided that the maker of the statement does not give evidence at the trial for one of the following reasons:

• the statement maker is dead or is physically or mentally unfit to give evidence. This extends the common rule which allowed hearsay only where the maker of a statement was dead or permanently insane;
• the statement maker is named and identified, but is outwith the United Kingdom and cannot reasonably be brought to court;
• the statement maker is named and identified, but cannot be found. Formerly, if a witness disappeared it was simply a misfortune which the litigant just had to put up with (*H.M. Advocate v. Monson* (1893) (hearsay of the writers was certainly not admissible));
• the statement maker refuses, whether lawfully or otherwise, to swear the oath or to give evidence in court. Section 261 of the Act provides that a co-accused who declines to give evidence may be treated as refusing to give evidence for the purposes of section 259. Taken together, these provisions partially overrule the effect of *McLay*. In most of the cases in which it is sought to lead evidence of a hearsay confession, the maker of the statement will refuse to give evidence, either because, as a co-accused in the same proceedings, he is entitled to do so, or because he simply refuses to do so or disappears altogether.

There are certain further preconditions which must also be satisfied before section 259 can operate:

- the person who made the statement will not give evidence in the proceedings for any of the reasons given above;
- evidence of the subject-matter of the statement would be admissible if the maker of the statement were to give direct oral evidence of it. There must, in other words, be no other exclusionary rule which affects the statement. For example, hearsay would not be admissible if a statement was privileged or constituted a precognition;
- the maker of the statement would have been a competent witness at the time the statement was made. This provision contrasts with those of the Civil Evidence (Scotland) Act 1988, which in permitting hearsay evidence do not specify the time at which the maker of the statement in question must be competent;
- there is sufficient evidence that a particular statement was made, and is either contained in a document or is one of which the person giving evidence about the statement has direct personal knowledge. This condition prevents the admission of "multiple" hearsay, which is permitted by the Civil Evidence (Scotland) Act 1988.

The rules about hearsay in criminal proceedings thus remain somewhat more restrictive than in civil cases, albeit that they have been considerably relaxed in comparison to the law stated in *McLay*.

6. In what circumstances may a witness be questioned about his or her sexual history? Do you regard the current rules on the matter as adequate? How might they be improved?

Model answer

Evidence about the sexual character of the complainer in a case involving sexual offences was at common law admissible to a limited extent. In *Dickie v. H.M. Advocate* (1897), it was held that while it was open to the accused to prove that the complainer was of "bad moral character", or to prove that "the witness voluntarily yielded to his embraces a short time before the alleged criminal attack", it was not permitted to prove individual acts of "unchastity". This view was in line with the law on character evidence in both civil and criminal cases. In general, character evidence is admissible—provided of course that it is relevant—where it deals with "general character", but not where the evidence relates to specific incidents displaying bad character. "General character" means simply the reputation of the witness as having certain characteristics of personality. The underlying rationale of the rule about sexual character was that evidence was admissible to attack the *credibility* of the witness, but not to suggest that "a female who yields her person to one man will presumably do so to any man—a proposition which is quite untenable".

In spite of the existence of such rules, questioning about the complainer's sexual history appears to have become common, in relation to the issues of both credibility *and* consent. The common technique was to suggest that the complainer was a person of loose habits or morals generally, or had behaved in a "provocative" way prior to the incident in question. The object was to suggest that the complainer was therefore likely to have consented in the particular case because she was likely to consent to sexual activity at any time, with anyone. The frequency of such attacks led to concern that victims of sexual assault were deterred from making complaints because of their fear of such sustained attempts to discredit them in court, and following a report by the Scottish Law Commission changes to the law were made in 1985 to restrict the extent to which such questioning would be permitted. Those changes are now embodied in sections 274 and 275 of the 1995 Act. The new provisions apply to more or less any case involving a sexual element, and prohibit questioning by any party other than the Crown designed to elicit evidence which shows or tends to show that the complainer is not of good character in relation to sexual matters, is a prostitute or associates with prostitutes, or has engaged in any sexual behaviour which does not form part of the charge. The Act provides a number of exceptions, however. Thus, questioning about sexual history or character is permitted where:

- the questioning is designed to rebut evidence led by someone other than the accused. This means that if the Crown attempt to show that the complainer is of particularly good sexual character, or was a virgin, something which is sometimes regarded as an aggravation to a charge of rape, then the accused may lead evidence in rebuttal;
- the questioning concerns sexual behaviour which took place on the same occasion as the sexual behaviour which is the subject of the charge. This reflects the idea expressed in *Dickie* that it would be relevant to show that the complainer had sexually "yielded" to the accused shortly before the alleged incident, or that it formed part of wider sexual context, such as participation in sexual behaviour as part of a group. It also accords with the common law notion of the *res gestae*—the idea that evidence is admissible about everything which happened on the same occasion, or as part of the same event.
- the questioning is relevant to a defence of incrimination. Here the accused is arguing that someone else was responsible for the sexual assault, and in order to make out that defence, clearly he may have to question the complainer as to whether she indulged in (or suffered) sexual behaviour with someone else;
- it would be contrary to the interests of justice to exclude the questioning. This exception is problematic, as it grants the court a wide discretion to admit evidence of sexual character where it sees fit to do so. A recent study indicates that in spite of the changes made in 1985, questioning about sexual character and history remains common (Brown, Burman and Jamieson, *Sex Crimes on Trial* (1992)). The 1995 Act introduced no changes to the substantive law in the light of this report.

There are few reported cases on these provisions. In *Bremner v. H.M. Advocate,* a rape case, the trial judge disallowed questioning about a relationship between the accused and the complainer which had ended some eight months prior to the incident. His decision was upheld on appeal, and although the High Court implied some reservations about the exclusion of the evidence in this case, they emphasised that the decision in such cases is very much a matter for the discretion of the trial judge and one which will not be reviewed except where the decision was not one which a reasonable judge could have made.

It is arguable that the present rules on sexual character evidence are unsatisfactory. In particular the "interests of justice" exception to the general prohibition of such evidence might be said to be so loosely drafted as to permit questioning in a very wide range of situations. Having said that, it is probably desirable and sensible to grant a discretion to the court to allow such evidence in exceptional cases, and it is difficult to envisage how that could be done in a form other than that adopted in the present legislation. The true view may be, therefore, that there is nothing wrong with the present law, but simply with the way it is operated by all who participate in the criminal justice process. In other words, a change in attitudes to the relevance of such evidence may be what is required, not a change in the law.

Author's note
These sample questions are adapted from questions set in the Ordinary Evidence Course at the University of Edinburgh between 1993 and 1997. They are therefore based on the format and content of the lectures in that course alone. The nature and subject-matter of the sample questions reproduced here should not be taken to be representative of a typical evidence examination paper, either at the University of Edinburgh or in any other institution. The assistance of my colleagues, and in particular Professor Robert Black, in the preparation and revision of these questions and their model answers, is gratefully acknowledged. The views expressed in the model answers are ultimately mine alone.

INDEX

accomplices, as witnesses, 72
accountants, confidentiality, 64
accused, as witnesses, 70–72, 92–94
  character evidence, 51–53
additional evidence, appeals, 82–84
admissibility of evidence, 22–45
  character (*see* **character evidence**)
  children's statements to social workers, 79
  computer records, 27, 93
  expert evidence, 56
  hearsay (*see* **hearsay**)
  improperly obtained evidence, 4, 32–45
    civil cases, 45
    fairness, 33, 34, 37, 38, 39, 40, 44
    searches (*see* **searches**)
    statements (*see* **statements**)
    undercover operations, 37, 88–89
  precognitions, 79
admissions, 60–62
  civil cases, 60–61
  criminal cases, 61–62
adultery, self-incrimination, 64
affidavits, increased use, 2
age, accused, confessions, 42
agreements, 60–62
  civil cases, 60–61
  criminal cases, 61–62
appeals, 80–84
  basic rule, 80–81
  criminal cases, 82–84
    additional evidence, 82, 83–84
  fact and law, 81–82
arrests, admissibility of statements, 39
automatism, burden of proof, 10

bankers, confidentiality, 64
best evidence, 2, 22–25
  1988 Act, 80, 90–92
  civil cases, 24–25
  criminal cases, 23
  prior identifications, 31
  rule, 22
blood samples, 35
bodily samples, 35
bugging, admissibility of statements, 42–44, 88–89
burden of proof, 6–10
  criminal cases, 10
  defenders, 7
  effect, 8
  evidential burdens, 9
  insanity, 10
  proving negatives, 7

  provisional burdens, 9
  pursuers, 6, 87–88
  shifting burden, 9
  tactical burdens, 9, 16
byelaws, judicial knowledge, 60

cars, searches, 36
cautions, confessions, 40–42
character evidence, 49–53
  accused, 51–53
  complainers, 49
  sexual character, 50–51, 94–96
children, as witnesses, 74–76
  statements to social workers, admissibility, 79
circumstantial evidence, 2, 5–6
  circumstantial facts, 1
citizens advice bureaus, confidentiality, 63
civil evidence, 1988 Act, 76–80
  best evidence, 80, 90–92
  corroboration, 76–77
  documentary evidence, 80
  hearsay, 77–80
  and criminal evidence, 3
collateral evidence, 5, 45–49
  character (*see* **character evidence**)
  civil cases, 47
  other criminal acts, 48–49
common sense, and relevance, 4
computer records, admissibility, 27, 93
confessions, *see also* **statements**
  admissibility, 38–44
  as corroboration, 18–19
    special knowledge confessions, 19, 90
  hearsay, 29
confidentiality, *see* **privilege**
consent, searches, 37–38
consistorial causes, agreements, 61
contempt of court, journalists, 64
  standard of proof, 14
contributory negligence, burden of proof, 7
corroboration, 17–22, 86–87, 90
  1988 Act, 76–77
  basic rule, 17
  civil cases, 16
  confessions, 18–19
  distress, 18
  expert evidence, 58
  identification, 20
  Moorov doctrine, 20–22
criminal evidence, and civil evidence, 3
cross-examination, accused, 70
  co-accused, 71

97

death, presumption, 11–12
defenders, burden of proof, 7
dental impressions, 35
diminished responsibility, burden of
    proof, 10
   mens rea, 57
direct evidence, 2
distress, as corroboration, 18
DNA samples, 35
doctors, confidentiality, 64
documentary evidence, 2
   1988 Act, 80
   best evidence, 24
   confidentiality, 62–67
   recovery, 61
   specification, 62
   validity, presumption, 12
drunkenness, confessions, 42

English law, hearsay, 27–28, 85
   judicial knowledge, 60
evidence, admissibility (*see* **admissibility
    of evidence**)
   categories, 1–3
   circumstantial evidence, 2, 5–6
   circumstantial facts, 1
   direct and secondary, 2
   documentary (*see* **documentary
    evidence**)
   facts and opinions, 2
   nature of proof, 1
   parole, 2
   procedural facts, 2
   sufficiency (*see* **sufficiency of evidence**)
evidential facts, 1
expert evidence, 55–58
   admissibility, 56
   corroboration, 58
   establishing qualifications, 57
   factual basis for expert testimony, 57–58
   necessity, 55
   psychological evidence, 56

facta probanda, 1
facta probationis, 1
facts in issue, 1
fairness, confessions, 38, 39, 40, 44
   improper searches, admissibility, 33, 34
   undercover operations, 37
fingerprints, 35
foreign law, judicial knowledge, 60
fraud, privileged information, 63

guilty pleas, 61

hearsay, 2, 25–32
   1988 Act, 77–80
    precognitions, 79
    statements bearing on credibility, 80

   confessions, 29
   Criminal Justice (Scotland) Act 1995,
    29–30
   English law, 27–28, 85
   evolution, 27
   meaning, 25
   previous identifications, 30–32
   primary and secondary, 25, 84–86
   prior statements, adoption, 30
   res gestae, 28
   self-serving statements, 29
homosexuality, and paedophilia, 4

identifications, 20
   Moorov doctrine, 21
   previous identifications, 30–32
immunity, accomplices, 72
   public interest immunity, 62, 66–67
incidental facts, 2
incrimination, defence, 51
innocence, presumption, 11
insanity, burden of proof, 10
   presumption of sanity, 10
   standard of proof, 15

journalists, confidentiality of sources, 64
judicial knowledge, 58–60

lawyers, confidentiality, 62–63

marital communications, confidentiality, 64
   privilege, 73
marriage guidance counselling,
    confidentiality, 63
mens rea, children under 8, 11
   vulnerable persons, 56, 57
mental disability, confessions, 42
miscarriages of justice, appeals, 82–84
Moorov doctrine, 20–22
   and collateral evidence, 47

onus of proof *see* **burden of proof**
opinion evidence, 2, 54–58
   expert opinion (*see* **expert evidence**)
   facts and opinions, 54
   'ultimate issue' rule, 54
ownership, presumption, 12

paedophilia, and homosexuality, 4
parole evidence, 2
paternity, presumption, 12
perjury, *res judicata*, 69
possession, recent possession, presump-
    tion, 12
precognitions, admissibility, 79
presumptions, 10–13
   activating, 11
   documents, validity, 12
   fact (*see* **presumptions of fact**)

innocence, 11
law (*see* **presumptions of law**)
rebuttable, 11
sanity, 10, 11
presumptions of fact, 10
recent possession, 12
res ipsa loquitur, 13
presumptions of law, 10–11
child-bearing, 12
death, 11–12
legitimacy, 12
ownership of moveable property, 12
succession, 12
previous convictions, admissibility, 5, 52
priests, confidentiality, 64
primary evidence, 2
private prosecutions, *res judicata,* 69
privilege, 62–67
communications *post litem motam,* 64
legal advisers, 62–63
marital communications, 64, 73
negotiations, 65
professional relations, 63–64
public interest immunity, 66–67
self-incrimination, 64
'without prejudice' communications, 65
probability, 1
procedural facts, 2
proof, *see also* **burden of proof;**
 standard of proof
nature, 13
public interest immunity, 62, 66–67
pursuers, burden of proof, 6, 87–88

relevance, 4
collateral evidence, 5
degrees, 46
likelihood of prejudice, 5
remoteness, 5
res gestae, 51
hearsay evidence, 28
res ipsa loquitur, 13
res judicata, 67–70
civil and criminal cases, 69–70
civil cases, 68–69
criminal cases, 69
private prosecutions, 69

Scots law, judicial knowledge, 60
searches, 33–37
bodily searches and samples, 35
consent, 37–38
fishing, 35
stumbling, 35
without warrants, 36

search warrants, 33
defects, 34
secondary evidence, 2
self-incrimination, accomplices, 72
admissibility, 38–44, 92–94
privilege, 64
sexual offences, distress, corroboration, 18
relevance, sexual history, 4, 50–51, 94–96
similar fact evidence, 5, 45
socii crimini, as witnesses, 72
spouses, as witnesses, 73
communications, privilege, 64, 73
standard of proof, 13–15
civil cases, 14
criminal cases, 15
insanity, 15
statements, admissibility, 38–44, 92–94
accidentally overheard, 43
bugging, 42–44, 88–89
cautions, 40–42
drunkenness, 42
fairness, 38, 39, 40, 89
inducements, 44, 88–89
threats, 44
vulnerable persons, 42
meaning, 78
prior statements, adoption, 30
statutory instruments, judicial knowledge, 60
succession, presumption, 12
sufficiency of evidence, 15–22
civil cases, 16
corroboration (*see* **corroboration**)
no case to answer, 16

testimonial evidence, 2
tholed assizes, 67, 69
trauma, children's evidence, 75–76
T.V. links, children's evidence, 76

undercover operations, 37

VAT, failure to pay, standard of proof, 15
video recordings, children's evidence, 76
volenti non fit injuria, burden of proof, 7
vulnerable persons, confessions, 42
psychological evidence, 56
witnesses, children, 75–76

witnesses, 70–76
accomplices, 72
accused, 70–71
children, 74–76
co-accused, 71, 92–94
spouses, 73